Greek
phrase book

AA Publishing

Contents

English edition prepared by First Edition Translations Ltd, Great Britain

Designed and produced by AA Publishing

First published in 1995 as Wat & Hoe Grieks, © Uitgeverij Kosmos bv - Utrecht/Antwerpen

Van Dale Lexicografie bv - Utrecht/Antwerpen

This edition © Automobile Association Developments Limited 1997
Reprinted Sep 1998
Reprinted Oct 1999
Reprinted Feb 2000
Reprinted Sep 2001
Reprinted Aug 2002
Reprinted Nov 2003
Reprinted May and Dec 2004
Reprinted Apr 2005
Reprinted Apr 2006

A CIP catalogue record for this book is available from the British Library

Published by AA Publishing (a trading name of Automobile Association Developments Limited, whose registered office is Fanum House, Basing View, Basingstoke, Hampshire RG21 4EA. Registered number 1878835).

A02932

Typeset by Anton Graphics Ltd, Andover, Hampshire.

Printed and bound in Italy by Printer Trento S.r.l.

Find out more about AA Publishing and the wide range of services the AA provides by visiting our web site at www.theAA.com/bookshop

Introduction

● **Welcome to the AA's new Essential Phrase Books series, covering the most popular European languages and containing everything you'd expect from a comprehensive language series. They're concise, accessible and easy to understand, and you'll find them indispensable on your trip abroad.**

Each guide is divided into 15 themed sections and starts with a pronunciation table which gives you the phonetic spelling to all the words and phrases you'll need to know for your trip, while at the back of the book is an extensive word list and grammar guide which will help you construct basic sentences in your chosen language.

Throughout the book you'll come across coloured boxes with a 🖑 beside them. These are designed to help you if you can't understand what your listener is saying to you. Hand the book over to them and encourage them to point to the appropriate answer to the question you are asking.

Other coloured boxes in the book - this time without the symbol - give alphabetical listings of themed words with their English translations beside them.

For extra clarity, we have put all English words and phrases in black, foreign language terms in red and their phonetic pronunciation in italic.

This phrase book covers all subjects you are likely to come across during the course of your visit, from reserving a room for the night to ordering food and drink at a restaurant and what to do if your car breaks down or you lose your traveller's cheques and money. With over 2,000 commonly used words and essential phrases at your fingertips you can rest assured that you will be able to get by in all situations, so let the Essential Phrase Book become your passport to a secure and enjoyable trip!

Pronunciation table

The sounds of Greek are not particularly easy for an English speaker. In the pronunciation guide given for each word or phrase, the following system is used:

a	somewhere between southern English **a** in **mast** and **u** in **cup**
b	similar to an English **b** but less aggressive
ch	as Scots **ch** in **loch**
d	similar to an English **d** but less agressive
dh	as English **th** in **the**, **this**, **them**
e	as English **e** in **met**
f	as English **f** in **soft**
g	as English **g** in **go**
gh	a difficult sound: try saying a hard English **g** (as in **grab**) as far down your throat as possible.
h	a more breathy form of the English **h** in **hoot**
i	like the **ee** in **feet**, but make the sound more clipped
k	like the English **c** in **cat**
l	as English **l** in **lick**
m	as English **m** in **mat**
n	as English **n** in **not**
ng	just like the **ng** in **English**
o	like the English **o** in **pop**
oo	like the **oo** in English **ooze**
p	a lot less explosive than an English **p**
r	lightly rolled, as in Italian or Scots: keep your tongue much closer to the back of your teeth than in a English **r**
s	as in English **sit**
t	more or less as in English **tap**
th	as English soft **th** in **thistle**
v	as in English **van**
w	as in English **went**
x	as the **x** in **box**
y	not a vowel but a glide, as in **yes**, **you**, **yacht**
z	as in English **zoo** or the **s** at the end of **was**

Note also the following combinations:

n(g)x	somewhere between English **things** and **thinks**
n(g)ch	as in the middle of **melancholy**

Stress and accents

In the pronunciation guide the stresses are marked with an accent, e.g. **o patéras** (father). The vowel **ou** is transcribed as **oo** when not stressed and **óo** when stressed. Any two other vowels together in the transcription must be pronounced separately, e.g. **aerodhrómyo** must be pronounced **a-e-rodhrómyo**, as must **oó**, which indicates two independent adjacent **o** sounds.

Useful lists

Useful lists

.1 Today or tomorrow?

What day is it today? _____	Τί μέρα είναι σήμερα;
	Ti méra íne símera?
Today's Monday _____	Σήμερα είναι Δευτέρα
	Símera íne dheftéra
– Tuesday _____	Σήμερα είναι Τρίτη
	Símera íne tríti
– Wednesday _____	Σήμερα είναι Τετάρτη
	Símera íne tetárti
– Thursday _____	Σήμερα είναι Πέμπτη
	Símera íne pémpti
– Friday _____	Σήμερα είναι Παρασκευή
	Símera íne paraskeví
– Saturday _____	Σήμερα είναι Σάββατο
	Símera íne sávato
– Sunday _____	Σήμερα είναι Κυριακή
	Símera íne kiriakí
in January _____	τον Ιανουάριο
	ton yanooário
since February _____	από το Φεβρουάριο
	apó to fevrooário
in spring _____	την άνοιξη
	tin ánixi
in summer _____	το καλοκαίρι
	to kalokyéri
in autumn _____	το φθινόπωρο
	to fthinóporo
in winter _____	το χειμώνα
	to himóna
1997 _____	χίλια εννιακόσια εννενήντα εφτά
	hília enyakósia enenínda eftá
the twentieth century _____	τον εικοστό αιώνα
	ton ikostó eóna
What's the date today? ____	Τί ημερομηνία έχουμε σήμερα/Πόσες του μηνός έχουμε σήμερα;
	ti imerominía éhome símera/póses too minós éhome símera?
Today's the 24th _____	Σήμερα είναι 24 του μηνός
	símera íne ikositéseres too minós
Monday 8 November 1998	Δευτέρα, 8 Νοεμβρίου 1998
	dheftéra ochtó noemvríoo hília enyakósia enenínda ochtó
in the morning _____	το πρωί
	to proí
in the afternoon _____	το μεσημέρι
	to mesiméri
in the evening _____	το βράδυ
	to vrádhi
at night _____	τη νύχτα
	ti níchta
this morning _____	σήμερα το πρωί
	símera to proí

this afternoon _____	σήμερα το μεσημέρι
	símera to mesiméri
this evening _____	σήμερα το απόγευμα
	símera to apóyevma
tonight _____	απόψε
	apópse
last night _____	την περασμένη νύχτα
	timberasméni níchta
this week _____	αυτή την εβδομάδα
	avtí tin evdhomádha
next month _____	τον επόμενο μήνα
	ton epómeno mína
last year _____	πέρυσι
	périsi
next... _____	τον επόμενο.../την επόμενη.../το επόμενο...
	ton epómeno.../tin epómeni.../to epómeno...
in...days/weeks/ _____	σε...μέρες/εβδομάδες/μήνες/χρόνια
months/years	*se...méres/evdhomádhes/hrónia*
...weeks ago _____	πριν από... εβδομάδες
	prin apó...evdhomádhes
day off _____	αργία
	aryía

1 .2 Bank holidays

● **The most important** public holidays in Greece are the following:

January 1	(New Year's Day) Η Πρωτοχρονιά
January 6	(Epiphany) Τα Επιφάνια
March 25	(The anniversary of the start of the War of Independence against the Turks in 1826) Εικοστή Πέμπτη Μαρτίου
April/May	(Easter: Greek Easter is celebrated according to the Orthodox Church calendar, and occurs on different dates from British Easter) Πάσχα
May 1	(May Day, Labour Day) Πρωτομαγιά
May/June	(Ascension; Whit Sunday) Της Αναλήψεως
August 15	(Assumption) Η Κοίμησις της Θεοτόκου
October 28	("No! Day": the day on which the Greeks refused the Italian ultimatum in 1940) Εικοστή Ογδόη Οκτωβρίου
December 25	(Christmas) Χριστούγεννα

Most shops, banks and government institutions are closed on these days. Good Friday and Boxing Day are not bank holidays.

1 .3 What time is it?

What time is it? _____	Τί ώρα είναι;
	ti óra íne?
It's nine o'clock _____	Είναι εννιά
	íne enyá
– five past ten _____	Είναι δέκα και πέντε
	íne dhéka ke pénde
– a quarter past eleven _____	Είναι έντεκα και τέταρτο
	íne éndeka ke tétarto
– twenty past twelve _____	Είναι δώδεκα και είκοσι
	íne dhódheka ke íkosi

9

– half past one	Είναι μιάμιση
	íne myámisi
– twenty-five to three	Είναι τρεις παρά είκοσι πέντε
	íne tris pará íkosi pénde
– a quarter to four	Είναι τέσσερες παρά τέταρτο
	íne téseres pará tétarto
– ten to five	Είναι πέντε παρά δέκα
	íne pénde pará dhéka
– twelve noon	Είναι δώδεκα το μεσημέρι
	íne dhódheka to mesiméri
– midnight	Είναι μεσάνυχτα
	íne mesánichta
half an hour	μισή ώρα
	misí óra
What time?	Τί ώρα;
	ti óra?
What time can I come round?	Τί ώρα μπορώ να περάσω;
	ti óra boró na peráso?
At...	Στις...
	stis...
After...	Μετά τις...
	metá tis...
Before...	Πριν από τις...
	prin apó tis...
Between...and...	Μεταξύ...και...
	metaxí... ke...
From...to...	Από τις...μέχρι τις...
	apó tis... méhri tis...
In...minutes	Σε...λεπτά
	se...leptá
– ...hours	Σε...ώρες
	se...óres
– a quarter of an hour	Σ΄ ένα τέταρτο
	s' éna tétarto
– three quarters of an hour	Σε τρία τέταρτα
	se tría tétarta
early	πολύ νωρίς
	polí norís
on time	στην ώρα
	stin óra
summertime	θερινή ώρα
	theriní óra
wintertime	χειμερινή ώρα
	himeriní óra

1 .4 One, two, three...

zero	μηδέν	*midhén*
1	ένα	*éna*
2	δύο	*dhío*
3	τρία	*tría*
4	τέσσερα	*téssera*
5	πέντε	*pénde*
6	έξι	*éxi*
7	εφτά	*eftá*
8	οχτώ	*ochtó*
9	εννιά	*enyá*

10	δέκα	dhéka
11	ένδεκα	éndheka
12	δώδεκα	dhódheka
13	δεκατρία	dhekatría
14	δεκατέσσερα	dhekatésera
15	δεκαπέντε	dhekapénde
16	δεκαέξι	dhekaéxi
17	δεκαεφτά	dhekaeftá
18	δεκαοχτό	dhekaochtó
19	δεκαεννιά	dekhaenyá
20	είκοσι	íkosi
21	είκοσι ένα	íkosi éna
22	είκοσι δύο	íkosi dhío
30	τριάντα	triánda
31	τριάντα ένα	triánda éna
32	τριάντα δύο	triánda dhío
40	σαράντα	saránda
50	πενήντα	penínda
60	εξήντα	exínda
70	εβδομήντα	evdhomínda
80	ογδόντα	oghdhónda
90	εννενήντα	enenínda
100	εκατό	ekató
101	εκατόν ένα	ekatón éna
110	εκατό δέκα	ekató dhéka
120	εκατόν είκοσι	ekatón íkosi
200	διακόσια	dhiakósia
300	τριακόσια	triakósia
400	τετρακόσια	tetrakósia
500	πεντακόσια	pendakósia
600	εξακόσια	exakósia
700	εφτακόσια	eftakósia
800	οχτακόσια	ochtakósia
900	εννιακόσια	enyakósia
1000	χίλια	hílya
1100	χίλια εκατό	hílya ekató
2000	δύο χιλιάδες	dhío hilyádhes
10,000	δέκα χιλιάδες	dhéka hilyádhes
100,000	εκατό χιλιάδες	ekató hilyádhes
1,000,000	ένα εκατομμύριο	éna ekatomírio
1st	πρώτος	prótos
2nd	δεύτερος	dhéfteros
3rd	τρίτος	trítos
4th	τέταρτος	tétartos
5th	πέμπτος	pémptos
6th	έκτος	éktos
7th	έβδομος	évdhomos
8th	όγδοος	óghdhoos
9th	ένατος	énatos
10th	δέκατος	dhékatos
11th	ενδέκατος	endhékatos
12th	δωδέκατος	dhodhékatos

13th	δέκατος τρίτος	*dhékatos trítos*
14th	δέκατος τέταρτος	*dhékatos tétartos*
15th	δέκατος πέμπτος	*dhékatos pémptos*
16th	δέκατος έκτος	*dhékatos éktos*
17th	δέκατος έβδομος	*dhékatos évdhomos*
18th	δέκατος όγδοος	*dhékatos óghdhoos*
19th	δέκατος ένατος	*dhékatos énatos*
20th	εικοστός	*ikostós*
21st	εικοστός πρώτος	*kostós prótos*
22nd	εικοστός δεύτερος	*ikostós dhéfteros*
30th	τριαντακοστός	*triandakostós*
100th	εκατοστός	*ekatostós*
1000th	χιλιοστός	*hilyostós*

once	μία φορά	*mía forá*
twice	δύο φορές	*dhío forés*
double	το διπλό	*to dhipló*
triple	το τριπλάσιο	*to triplásio*
half	το μισό	*to misó*
a quarter	ένα τέταρτο	*éna tétarto*
a third	ένα τρίτο	*éna tríto*
a few, some	μερικά	*meriká*

2+4=6	δύο και τέσσερα ίσον έξι	*dhío ke tésera íson éxi*
4-2=2	τέσσερα μείον δύο ίσον δύο	*tésera míon dhío íson dhío*
2x4=8	δύο επί τέσσερα ίσον οχτώ	*dhío epí tésera íson ochtó*
4÷2=2	τέσσερα διά δύο ίσον δύο	*tésera dhía dhío íson dhío*
odd/even	μονός/ζυγός	*mónos/zighós*
total	συνολικά	*sinoliká*
6x9	έξι επί εννιά	*éxi epí enyá*

.5 The weather

Is the weather going to be good/bad?	Θα έχουμε καλό/κακό καιρό; *tha éhoome kaló/kakó kyeró?*
Is it going to get colder/hotter?	Θα κάνει περισσότερο κρύο/περισσότερη ζέστη; *tha káni perisótero krío/perisóteri zésti?*
What temperature is it going to be today?	Τί θερμοκρασία θα κάνει σήμερα; *ti thermokrasía tha káni símera?*
Is it going to rain?	Θα βρέξει; *tha vréxi?*

Is there going to be a storm?	Θα έχουμε θύελλα;
	tha éhoome thíela?
Is it going to snow?	Θα χιονίσει;
	tha hyonísi?
Is it going to freeze?	Θα κάνει παγωνιά;
	tha káni pagonyá?
Is the thaw setting in?	Θα λιώσουν τα χιόνια;
	tha lyósoon ta hyónya?
Is it going to be foggy?	Θα πέσει ομίχλη;
	tha pési omíchli?
Is there going to be a thunderstorm?	Θα έχουμε καταιγίδα;
	tha éhoome kateyídha?
The weather's changing	Αλλάζει ο καιρός
	alázi o kyerós
It's cooling down	Δροσίζει
	dhrosízi
What's the weather going to be like today/tomorrow?	Τί καιρό θα έχουμε σήμερα/αύριο;
	ti kyéro tha éhoome símera/ávrio?

.6 Here, there...

See also 5.1 Asking for directions

here/there	εδώ/εκεί
	edhó/ekí
somewhere/nowhere	κάπου/πουθενά
	kápoo/poothená
everywhere	παντού
	pandóo
far away/nearby	μακριά/κοντά
	makriá/kondá
to the right/left	προς τα δεξιά/αριστερά
	pros ta dhexyá/aristerá
on the right/left of	δεξιά/αριστερά από
	dhexyá/aristerá apó
straight ahead	ίσια
	ísya
via	μέσω
	méso
in	σε
	se
on	πάνω σε
	páno se
under	κάτω από
	káto apó
against	εναντίον
	enandíon
opposite	απέναντι
	apénandi
next to/near	δίπλα σε/κοντά σε
	dhípla se/kondá se
in front of	μπροστά
	brostá
in the centre	στη μέση
	sti mési

άνεμος **wind**	ελαφρές νεφώσεις **light cloud**	ομίχλη **mist/fog**
ανέφελος **cloudless**	ζεστός **hot**	παγετός **frost**
αποπνικτικός **muggy/** **oppressive**	ηλιόλουστο **sunny**	ριπές αέρα **gusts of wind**
αφόρητη ζέστη **unbearable heat**	θύελλα **storm**	συννεφιά **cloudy**

...βαθμοί κάτω/πάνω
  από το μηδέν
...degrees
  below/above
  zero
	καλός
	fine
	καύσωνας
	heatwave
		τσουχτερός
		bitingly
		  cold
		τυφώνας
		cyclone

βαριές νεφώσεις **heavy cloud**	μαλακός/ήπιος **mild**	φυσάει **it is windy**
βροχερός **damp**	μέτριος/δυνατός άνεμος **medium/strong**	χαλάζι **hail**
βροχή **rain**	**winds**	χιόνι **snow**
δροσερός **cool**	μισοσυννεφιασμένος **partly cloudy** μπόρα **squall of rain**	ψυχρός **very cold**

forward_____	εμπρός/προς τα εμπρός *embrós/pros ta embrós*
down_____	(προς τα) κάτω *(pros ta) káto*
up_____	(προς τα) πάνω *(pros ta) páno*
inside _____	(προς τα) μέσα *(pros ta) mésa*
outside _____	(προς τα) έξω *(pros ta) éxo*
behind _____	(προς τα) πίσω *(pros ta) píso*
at the front _____	μπροστά *brostá*
at the back_____	πίσω - πίσω *píso-píso*
in the north _____	στο βορρά *sto vorá*
to the south_____	προς το νότο *pros to nóto*
from the west_____	από τη δύση *apó ti dhísi*
from the east _____	της ανατολής *tis anatolís*
north/south/west/east of ___	βόρεια/νότια/δυτικά/ ανατολικά από *vórya/nótya/dhitiká/ anatolitiká apó*

.7 What does that sign say?

See also 5.4 Traffic signs.

ΑΝΔΡΩΝ gents	ΕΛΕΥΘΕΡΗ ΕΙΣΟΔΟΣ free entry	ΠΡΟΣΟΧΗ ΒΑΦΗ wet paint
ΑΝΕΛΚΥΣΤΗΡΑΣ lift	ΕΝΟΙΚΙΑΖΕΤΑΙ to let	ΠΡΟΣΟΧΗ ΣΚΥΛΟΣ beware of the dog
ΑΝΟΙΧΤΟ/ΚΛΕΙΣΤΟ open/shut	ΕΞΟΔΟΣ exit	ΠΡΟΣΟΧΗ ΤΟ ΣΚΑΛΙ mind the step
ΑΠΑΓΟΡΕΥΕΤΑΙ Η ΕΙΣΟΔΟΣ no entry	ΕΞΟΔΟΣ ΚΙΝΔΥΝΟΥ emergency exit	ΠΡΩΤΕΣ ΒΟΗΘΕΙΕΣ accident and
ΑΠΑΓΟΡΕΥΕΤΑΙ Η ΦΩΤΟΓΡΑΦΗΣΗ no photography	ΙΔΙΟΚΤΗΣΙΑ private/private property	emergency service ΠΩΛΕΙΤΑΙ for sale
ΑΠΑΓΟΡΕΥΕΤΑΙ ΝΑ ΠΑΤΑΤΕ ΣΤΟ ΓΡΑΣΙΔΙ do not walk on the grass	ΚΙΝΔΥΝΟΣ danger ΚΙΝΔΥΝΟΣ ΘΑΝΑΤΟΥ danger! ΚΙΝΔΥΝΟΣ	ΡΕΣΕΨΙΟΝ reception ΣΗΜΑ ΚΙΝΔΥΝΟΥ emergency cord/alarm button
ΑΠΑΓΟΡΕΥΕΤΑΙ ΤΟ ΚΑΠΝΙΣΜΑ no smoking	ΠΥΡΚΑΓΙΑΣ fire hasard ΚΛΕΙΣΜΕΝΟ/	ΣΚΑΛΑ stairs ΣΚΑΛΑ ΠΥΡΚΑΓΙΑΣ
ΑΠΑΓΟΡΕΥΟΝΤΑΙ ΤΑ ΚΑΤΟΙΚΙΔΙΑ ΖΩΑ no pets	ΡΕΖΕΡΒΕ booked/reserved ΚΥΛΙΟΜΕΝΗ	fire escape ΣΥΡΑΤΕ/ΩΘΗΣΑΤΕ pull/push
ΑΠΟΧΩΡΗΤΗΡΙΑ/ ΤΟΥΑΛΕΤΤΕΣ lavatories/toilets	ΣΚΑΛΑ escalator ΜΗ ΠΟΣΙΜΟ ΝΕΡΟ	ΤΑΜΕΙΟ cash desk/booking office
ΓΥΝΑΙΚΩΝ ladies	no drinking water ΜΗΝ ΑΓΓΙΖΕΤΕ	ΥΓΡΟ damp
ΕΔΩ ΠΛΗΡΟΦΟΡΙΕΣ information desk	do not touch ΜΗΝ ΕΝΟΧΛΕΙΤΕ do not disturb	ΥΨΗΛΗ ΤΑΣΙΣ high tension cables/high voltage
ΕΙΣΟΔΟΣ entrance	ΟΡΟΦΟΣ floor	ΞΕΠΟΥΛΗΜΑ clearance sale
ΕΚΠΤΩΣΕΙΣ reduction/sale	ΠΛΗΡΕΣ full	ΩΡΕΣ ΛΕΙΤΟΥΡΓΙΑΣ
ΕΚΤΟΣ ΛΕΙΤΟΥΡΓΙΑΣ out of order	ΠΛΗΡΟΦΟΡΙΕΣ information	opening hours

.8 Telephone alphabet

α	_____ *álfa*	Αλέξανδρος	Aléxandhros
β	_____ *víta*	Βασίλιος	Vasílyos
γ	_____ *gháma*	Γεώργιος	Yeóryos
δ	_____ *dhélta*	Δημήτριος	Dhimítrios
ε	_____ *épsilon*	Ελένη	Eléni
ζ	_____ *zíta*	Ζωή	Zoí

15

Useful lists

η_____	íta	Ηρακλής	Iraklís
θ_____	thíta	Θεόδωρος	Theódhoros
ι_____	yóta	Ιωάννης	Yoánis
κ_____	kápa	Κωνσταντίνος	Konstandínos
λ_____	lámdha	Λεωνίδας	Leonídhas
μ_____	mi	Μενέλαος	Menélaos
ν_____	ni	Νικόλαος	Nikólaos
ξ_____	xi	Ξενοφών	Xenofón
ο_____	ómikron	Οδυσσέας	Odhiséas
π_____	pi	Περικλής	Periklís
ρ_____	ro	Ρόδος	Ródhos
σ_____	síghma	Σωτήριος	Sotiríos
τ_____	taf	Τιμολέων	Timoléon
υ_____	ípsilon	Υψηλάντης	Ipsilándis
φ_____	fi	Φώτιος	Fótyos
χ_____	hi	Χρήστος	Chrístos
ψ_____	psi	Ψάλτης	Psáltis
ω_____	omégha	Ωμέγα	Omégha

🄵.9 Personal details

surname_____	επώνυμο
	epónimo
christian name(s)_____	(μικρό) όνομα
	(mikró) ónoma
initials_____	τα αρχικά
	ta arhiká
address (street/number) ___	η διεύθυνση (οδός / αριθμός)
	idhiéfthinsi (odhós/arithmós)
post code/town _____	ταχυδρομικός κώδικας / αριθμός κατοικίας
	tahidhromikós kódhikas/tópos katikías
sex (male/female) _____	φύλο (άρρεν / θήλυ)
	fílo (áren/thíli)
nationality_____	υπηκοότητα
	ipikoótita
date of birth _____	ημερομηνία γεννήσεως
	imerominía yeníseos
place of birth _____	τόπος γεννήσεως
	tópos yeníseos

occupation_____	επάγγελμα
	epàngelma
married/single/divorced____	έγγαμος / άγαμος / διεζευγμένος
	éngamos/àgamos/dhiezevgménos
widowed _____	εν χηρεία
	en hiría
(number of) children _____	τέκνα (αριθμός τέκνων)
	tékna (arithmós téknon)
passport/identity _____	αριθμός ταυτότητας / διαβατηρίου / άδειας
card/driving licence	οδηγήσεως
number	*arithmós taftótitas / dhiavatíryoo/ádhias*
	odhiyíseos
place and date of issue ____	τόπος και ημερομηνία έκδοσης
	tópos ke imerominía ékdhosis

Courtesies

Courtesies

● **It is usual in Greece** for friends and relatives of both sexes to kiss each other on both cheeks when meeting and parting company. People who know each other less well shake hands instead.

.1 Greetings

Hello, Mr Smith _____ Γειά σας κύριε Σμιθ
ya sas kírie Smith

Hello, Mrs Jones _____ Γειά σας κυρία Ντζωνς
Ya sas kiría Jones

Hello, Peter _____ Γειά σου Πέτρο
ya soo Pétro

Hi, Helen _____ Γειά σου Ελένη
ya soo Eléni

Good morning, madam____ Καλημέρα κυρία
kaliméra kiría

Good afternoon, sir _____ Καλησπέρα κύριε
kalispéra kírie

Good evening_____ Καλησπέρα
kalispéra

How are you? _____ Τί κάνετε;
ti kánete

Fine, thank you, and you?__ Καλά, κι εσείς;
kalá kyesís?

Very well _____ Πολύ καλά
polí kalá

Not very well _____ Οχι και τόσο καλά
óhi ke tóso kalá

Not too bad_____ Ετσι κι έτσι...
étsi kyétsi

I'd better be going_____ Φεύγω τώρα
févgo tóra

I have to be going _____ Πρέπει να φύγω τώρα
prépi na fígo tóra

Someone's waiting _____ Με περιμένουν. Γεια σας !
for me Bye! *Me periménoon. Ya sas!*

Goodbye _____ Αντίο
adío

See you later _____ Θα σε δω αργότερα
tha se dho argótera

See you in a little while____ Θα σε δω σε λίγο
tha se dho se lígho

Sleep well _____ Καλό ύπνο
kaló ípno

Good night _____ Καληνύχτα
kaliníchta

All the best _____ Στο καλό να πας/όλα καλά
sto kaló na pas/ óla kalá

Have fun_____ Καλή διασκέδαση
kalí dhiaskédhasi

Good luck _____ Καλή επιτυχία
kalí epitihía

Have a nice holiday	Καλές διακοπές
	kalés dhiakopés
Have a good trip	Καλό ταξίδι
	kaló taxídhi
Thank you, you too	Ευχαριστώ, επίσης
	efharistó, epísis
Say hello to...for me	Χαιρετισμούς σε...
	heretizmóos se...

.2 How to ask a question

Who?	Ποιός
	pyós?
Who's that?	Ποιός είναι;
	pyós íne?
What?	Τί;
	ti?
What's there to see here?	Τί αξιοθέατα έχει εδώ;
	ti axiothéata éhi edhó?
What kind of hotel is that?	Τί είδος ξενοδοχείο είναι αυτό;
	ti ídhos xenodhohío íne aftó?
What time is it?	Τί ώρα είναι;
	ti óra íne?
Where?	Πού;
	poo?
Where's the toilet?	Πού είναι η τουαλέτα;
	poo íne i twaléta?
Where are you going?	Πού πηγαίνετε;
	poo piyénete?
Where are you from?	Από πού έρχεσθε;
	apó poo érhesthe?
How?	Πώς;
	pos?
How far is that?	Πόσο μακριά είναι;
	póso makriá íne?
How long does that take?	Πόση ώρα διαρκεί/κρατάει;
	pósi óra dhiarkí/kratái?
How long is the trip?	Πόσο κρατάει το ταξίδι;
	póso kratái to taxídhi?
How much?	Πόσος;
	pósos
How much is this?	Πόσο κάνει;
	póso káni?
Which?	Ποιό; Ποιά;
	pyo? pya?
Which glass is mine?	Ποιό ποτήρι είναι δικό μου;
	pyo potíri íne dhikó moo?
When?	Πότε;
	póte?
When are you leaving?	Πότε φεύγετε;
	póte févyete?
Why?	Γιατί;
	yatí?
Could you...me?	Μπορείτε να με... ;
	boríte na me...?
Could you help me, please?	Μπορείτε να με βοηθήσετε, παρακαλώ;
	boríte na me voithísete, parakaló?

Could you point that out to me?	Μπορείτε να μου το δείξετε; *boríte na moo to díhxete?*
Could you come with me, please?	Μπορείτε να 'ρθείτε μαζί μου, παρακαλώ; *boríte narthíte mazí moo, parakaló?*
Could you...	Θέλετε.../Μπορείτε... ; *thélete...?/Boríte...?*
Could you reserve some tickets for me, please?	Μπορείτε να μου κλείσετε εισιτήρια, παρακαλώ; *boríte na moo klísete isitíria parakaló?*
Do you know...?	Ξέρετε...; *xérete...?*
Do you know another hotel, please?	Μήπως ξέρετε κανένα άλλο ξενοδοχείο; *mípos xérete kanéna álo xenodhohío*
Do you have...?	Μήπως έχετε...; *mípos éhete...?*
Do you have a...?	Μπορείτε να μου δώσετε ένα...; *boríte na moo dhósete éna...?*
Do you have a vegetarian dish, please?	Μήπως έχετε φαγητό χωρίς κρέας; *mípos éhete faitó chorís kréas?*
I'd like...	Θα ήθελα... *tha íthela...*
I'd like a kilo of apples, please.	Θα ήθελα ένα κιλό μήλα *tha íthela éna kiló míla*
Can I...?	Μπορώ... ; *boró...?*
Can I take this?	Μπορώ να το πάρω μαζί μου; *boró na to páro mazí moo?*
Can I smoke here?	Μπορώ να καπνίσω εδώ; *boró na kapníso edhó?*
Could I ask you something?	Μπορώ να ρωτήσω κάτι; *boró na rotíso káti?*

.3 How to reply

Yes, of course	Ναι, βέβαια/Βεβαίως *ne, vévea/vevéos*
No, I'm sorry	Οχι, λυπάμαι *óhi, lipáme*
Yes, what can I do for you?	Ορίστε *oríste*
Just a moment, please	Μια στιγμή/Ένα λεπτό, παρακαλώ *mya stighmí/éna leptó parakaló*
No, I don't have time now	Οχι, δε με βολεύει τώρα *óhi dhen me volévi tóra*
No, that's impossible	Οχι, δε γίνεται *óhi, dhe yínete*
I think so	Νομίζω *nomízo*
I agree	Κι εγώ το νομίζω *kyeghó to nomízo*
I hope so too	Κι εγώ το ελπίζω *kyeghó to elpízo*
No, not at all	Οχι, καθόλου *óhi kathóloo*
No, no one	Οχι, κανένας *óhi kanénas*

No, nothing	Οχι, τίποτα
	óhi típota
That's (not) right	Ετσι είναι / (Δεν) είναι έτσι
	étsi íne/(dhen) íne étsi
I (don't) agree	(Δε) συμφωνώ μαζί σας
	(dhe) simfonó mazí sas
All right	Καλά
	kalá
Okay	Εντάξει
	endáxi
Perhaps	Ισως/Μπορεί
	ísos/borí
I don't know	Δεν ξέρω
	dhen xéro

.4 Thank you

Thank you	Ευχαριστώ
	efcharistó
You're welcome	Παρακαλώ
	parakaló
Thank you very much	Ευχαριστώ πολύ
	efcharistó polí
Very kind of you	Πολύ ευγενικό εκ μέρους σας
	polí evyenikó ek méroos sas
I enjoyed it very much	Χάρηκα πολύ
	Chárika polí
Thank you for your trouble	Ευχαριστώ για τον κόπο
	efcharistó ya tongópo
You shouldn't have	Δεν ήταν ανάγκη
	dhen ítan anángi
That's all right	Δεν πειράζει
	dhembirázi

.5 Sorry

Sorry!	Συγγνώμη
	sighnómi
Excuse me	Με συγχωρείτε
	me sinchoríte
I'm sorry, I didn't know...	Συγγνώμη, δεν ήξερα ότι...
	sighnómi dhen íxera óti...
I do apologise	Με συγχωρείτε
	me sinchoríte
I'm sorry	Λυπάμαι
	lipáme
I didn't do it on purpose, it was an accident	Δεν τό 'κανα επίτηδες, έγινε κατά λάθος
	dhen tókana epítidhes, éyine katá láthos
Never mind	Εντάξει έτσι
	endáxi étsi
It could've happened to anyone	Αυτό μπορεί να συμβεί στον καθένα
	aftó borí na simví stongathéna

.6 What do you think?

Which do you prefer?	Τί προτιμάτε;
	ti protimáte?
Do you like it?	Σου αρέσει;
	soo arési?
Don't you like dancing?	Δε σ' αρέσει να χορεύεις;
	dhe sarési na chorévis?
I don't mind	Το ίδιο μου κάνει
	to ídhyo moo káni
Well done!	Μπράβο!
	brávo
Not bad!	Οχι άσχημο!
	óhi áschimo!
Great!	Υπέροχο!
	ipérocho!
Wonderful!	Θαυμάσιο!
	thavmásio!
It's really nice here!	Τι ωραία που είναι εδώ!
	ti oréa poo íne edhó!
How nice!	Τι ωραίο!
	ti oréo!
How nice for you!	Χαίρομαι για σας!
	hérome ya sas!
I'm (not) very happy with...	(Δεν) είμαι πολύ ευχαριστημένος/ ευχαριστημένη με...
	(dhen) íme polí efcharistiménos/ efcharistiméni me...
I'm glad that...	Χαίρομαι που...
	hérome poo ...
I'm having a great time	Περνάω μια χαρά
	pernáo mya chará
I'm looking forward to it	Περιμένω ανυπόμονα
	periméno anipómona
I hope it'll work out	Ελπίζω να πετύχει
	elpízo na petíhi
What a mess!	Τί χάλια!
	ti hálya!
That's terrible!	Τί απαίσιο!
	ti apésyo!
What a pity!	Τί κρίμα!
	ti kríma!
That's filthy!	Τί αηδία!
	ti aidhía!
What a load of rubbish!	Τί ανοησίες/σαχλαμάρες!
	ti anoisíes/sachlamáres!
I don't like...	Δε μου αρέσει...
	dhe moo arési...
I'm bored to death	Πλήττω φοβερά...
	plíto foverá
I've had enough	Βαρέθηκα πια
	varéthika pya
I can't take any more of this	Δεν το ανέχομαι άλλο
	dhen to anéchome álo
I was expecting something completely different	Περίμενα κάτι τελείως διαφορετικό
	perímena káti telíos dhyaforetikó

Conversation

Conversation

3.1 I beg your pardon?

I don't speak any/ _____ I speak a little...	Δε μιλάω/μιλάω λίγα... *dhe miláo/miláo lígha...*
I'm English _____	Είμαι Άγγλος/Αγγλίδα *íme ánglos/anglídha*
I'm Scottish _____	Είμαι Σκωτσέζος/Σκωτσέζα *íme scotsézos/scotséza*
I'm Irish _____	Είμαι Ιρλανδός/Ιρλανδέζα *íme irlandhós/irlandhéza*
I'm Welsh _____	Είμαι Ουαλλός/Ουαλλή *íme walós/walí*
Do you speak _____ English/French/German?	Μιλάτε αγγλικά/γαλλικά/γερμανικά; *miláte angliká/ghaliká/yermaniká?*
Is there anyone who _____ speaks...?	Ξέρει κανείς εδώ... ; *xéri kanís edhó...?*
I beg your pardon? _____	Ορίστε;/Τι είπατε; *oríste?/ti ípate?*
I (don't) understand _____	(Δεν) καταλαβαίνω *(dhen) katalavéno*
Do you understand me? ___	Με καταλαβαίνετε; *me katalavénete?*
Could you repeat that, _____ please?	Μπορείτε να το επαναλάβετε, παρακαλώ; *boríte na to epanalávete, parakaló?*
Could you speak more _____ slowly, please?	Μπορείτε να μιλάτε πιο αργά, παρακαλώ; *boríte na miláte pyo arghá, parakaló?*
What does that (word) _____ mean?	Τί θα πει αυτό/αυτή η λέξη; *ti tha pi aftó/aftí i léxi?*
Is that similar to/the _____ same as...?	Είναι (περίπου) το ίδιο με... ; *íne (perípoo) to ídhyo me...?*
Could you write that _____ down for me, please?	Μου το γράφετε, παρακαλώ; *moo to ghráfete, parakaló?*
Could you spell that _____ for me, please?	Μου το συλλαβίζετε, παρακαλώ; *moo to silavízete, parakaló?*

(See 1.8 Telephone alphabet)

Could you point that _____ out in this phrase book, please?	Μπορείτε να το δείξετε σ' αυτό τον οδηγό; *boríte na to díxete saftó tonodhighó?*
One moment, please, _____ I have to look it up	Ένα λεπτό, πρέπει να το ψάξω πρώτα *éna leptó, prépi na to psáxo próta*
I can't find the word/the ___ sentence	Δεν μπορώ να βρω τη λέξη/τη φράση *dhemboró na vro ti léxi/ti frási*
How do you say _____ that in...?	Πώς λέγεται αυτό στα... ; *pos léyete aftó sta...?*
How do you pronounce _____ that?	Πώς προφέρεται αυτό; *pos proférete aftó?*

May I introduce myself?	Επιτρέψτε μου να συστηθώ
	epitrépste moo na sistithó
My name's...	Λέγομαι.../Με λένε...
	léghome.../me léne...
I'm...	Είμαι...ο/η
	íme...o/i
What's your name?	Πώς λέγεσθε; / Πώς σας λένε;
	pos léyesthe?/ pos sas léne?
May I introduce...?	Επιτρέψτε μου να σας συστήσω
	epitrépste moo na sas sistíso
This is my wife/ daughter/mother/ girlfriend	Αυτή είναι η γυναίκα μου/η κόρη μου/η μητέρα μου/η φίλη μου
	aftí íne i yinéka moo/i kóri moo/i mitéra moo/i fíli moo
– my husband/son/ father/boyfriend	Αυτός είναι ο άντρας μου/ο γιός μου/ο πατέρας μου/ο φίλος μου
	aftós íne o ándras moo/ o yos moo/o patéras moo/o fílos moo
How do you do	Γειά σας, χαίρομαι για τη γνωριμία σας
	ya sas, hérome ya ti ghnorimía sas
Pleased to meet you	Χαίρω πολύ
	héro polí
Where are you from?	Από πού είστε;
	apó poo íste?
I'm from England/Scotland/ Ireland/Wales	Είμαι απ' την Αγγλία/τη Σκωτία/την Ιρλανδία/την Ουαλία
	íme apó tin anglía/ti scotía/ tin irlandhía/tin walía
What city do you live in?	Σε ποιά πόλη μένετε;
	se pya póli ménete?
In..., it's near...	Σε...Είναι κοντά σε...
	se...íne kondá se
Have you been here long?	Είστε πολύ καιρό εδώ;
	íste polí keró edhó?
A few days	Μερικές μέρες
	merikés méres
How long are you staying here?	Πόσο καιρό θα μείνετε εδώ;
	póso kyeró tha mínete edhó?
We're (probably) leaving tomorrow/in two weeks	(Μάλλον) θα φύγουμε αύριο/σε δύο εβδομάδες
	(málon) tha fíghoome ávrio/se dhío evdhomádhes
Where are you staying?	Που μένετε;
	poo ménete?
In a hotel/an apartment	Σ' ένα ξενοδοχείο/σε διαμέρισμα
	séna xenodhohío/se dhiamérizma
On a camp site	Σ' ένα κάμπινγκ
	séna kámping
With friends/relatives	Σε φίλους/σε συγγενείς
	se fíloos/se singenís
Are you here on your own/with your family?	Είστε μόνος σας /μόνη σας /με την οικογένειά σας;
	íste mónos sas/móni sas/me tin ikoyényásas?

English	Greek	Pronunciation
I'm on my own	Είμαι μόνος μου /μόνη μου	íme mónos moo/móni moo
I'm with my partner/wife/husband	Είμαι με το /τη σύντροφό μου/τη γυναίκα μου/τον άντρα μου	íme me to/ti síndtrofómoo/ti yinéka moo/ton ándra moo
– with my family	Είμαι με την οικογένειά μου	íme me tin ikoyéniámoo
– with relatives	Είμαι με συγγενείς μου	íme me singenís moo
– with a friend/friends	Είμαι μ' ένα φίλο/με μία φίλη/με φίλους	íme ména fílo/me mya fíli/me fíloos
Are you married?	Είστε παντρεμένος/παντρεμένη;	íste pandreménos/pandreméni?
Do you have a steady boyfriend/girlfriend?	Έχεις ένα φίλο/μια φιλενάδα;	éhis éna fílo/mya filenádha?
That's none of your business	Δε σας ενδιαφέρει/Δε σας πέφτει λόγος	dhe sas endhiaféri/dhe sas péfti lóghos
I'm married	Είμαι παντρεμένος/παντρεμένη	íme pandreménos/pandreméni
– single	Είμαι εργένης	íme eryénis
– separated	Είμαι χωρισμένος/χωρισμένη (από κλίνη και στέγη)	íme chorizménos/chorizméni (apó klíni ke stéyi)
– divorced	Είμαι διεζευγμένος/διεζευγμένη	íme dhiezevghménos/dhiezevghméni
– a widow/widower	Είμαι χήρα/χήρος	íme híra/híros
I live alone/with someone (m)/someone (f)	Μένω μόνος μου/μόνη μου/μαζί με το φίλο μου/τη φιλενάδα μου	méno mónos moo/móni moo/mazí me to fílo moo/ti filenádha moo
Do you have any children/grandchildren?	Έχετε παιδιά/εγγόνια;	éhete pedhyá/engónya?
How old are you?	Πόσων χρονών είστε;	póson chronón íste?
How old is she/he?	Πόσων χρονών είναι;	póson chronón íne?
I'm...	Είμαι...χρονών	íme...chronón
She's/he's...	Είναι...χρονών	íne...chronón
What do you do for a living?	Τί δουλειά κάνετε;	ti dhoolyá kánete?
I work in an office	Δουλεύω σ' ένα γραφείο	dhoolévo séna ghrafío
I'm a student/ I'm at school	Σπουδάζω/πηγαίνω σχολείο	spoodházo/piyéno scholío
I'm unemployed	Είμαι άνεργος/άνεργη	íme ánerghos/áneryi
I'm retired	Είμαι συνταξιούχος/συνταξιούχα	íme sintaxióochos/sintaxióocha
I'm on a disability pension	Είμαι ανίκανος/ανίκανη για εργασία, έχω επίδομα ανικανότητας	íme aníkanos/aníkani ya erghasía, ého epídhoma anikanótitas

I'm a housewife _____	Είμαι νοικοκυρά
	íme nikokirá
Do you like your job? _____	Σας αρέσει η δουλειά σας;
	sas arési i dhoolyásas?
Most of the time _____	Μερικές φορές ναι, μερικές φορές όχι
	merikés forés ne, merikés forés óhi
I usually do, but I prefer ___	Συνήθως μ' αρέσει, αλλά οι διακοπές μ'
holidays	αρέσουν πιο πολύ
	siníthos marési,alá i dhiakopés marésoon
	pyo polí

3 .3 Starting/ending a conversation

Could I ask you _____ something?	Μπορώ να σας ρωτήσω κάτι;
	boró na sas rotíso káti?
Excuse me_____	Με συγχωρείτε
	me sinchoríte
Excuse me, could you _____ help me?	Συγγνώμη, μήπως μπορείτε να με βοηθήσετε;
	signómi, mípos boríte na me voithísete?
Yes, what's the problem? __	Ναι, ποιό είναι το πρόβλημά σας;
	ne, pyo íne to próvlimásas?
What can I do for you? ____	Τί μπορώ να κάνω για σας;
	ti boró na káno ya sas?
Sorry, I don't have time____ now	Λυπάμαι, δεν έχω καιρό τώρα
	lipáme, dhen écho keró tóra
Do you have a light? _____	Μήπως έχετε φωτιά;
	mípos éhete fotyá?
May I join you? _____	Μπορώ να καθίσω δίπλα σας;
	boró na kathíso dhípla sas?
Could you take a _____ picture of me/us? Press this button	Μπορείτε να με/μας βγάλετε μια φωτογραφία; Να πιέστε αυτό το κουμπί
	boríte na me/mas vghálete mya fotografía?
	na pyéste avtó to koobí
Leave me alone _____	Ασε με ήσυχο
	áse me ísicho
Get lost_____	Εξαφανίσου
	exafanísoo
Go away or I'll scream_____	Αν δε φύγετε, θα βάλω τις φωνές
	an dhe fíyete, tha válo tis fonés

3 .4 Congratulations and condolences

Happy birthday/many_____ happy returns	Χρόνια πολλά
	chrónya polá
Please accept my_____ condolences	Τα συλλυπητήριά μου
	ta silipitíryámoo
I'm very sorry for you _____	Ηταν μεγάλο πλήγμα
	ítan meghálo plíghma

3 .5 A chat about the weather

See also 1.5 The weather

It's so hot/cold today!_____	Τί ζέστη/κρύο που κάνει σήμερα!
	ti zésti/krío poo káni símera!
Nice weather, isn't it? _____	Τί ωραίος καιρός, ε;
	ti oréos kerós, e?

What a wind/storm! _____	Τί αέρας/θύελλα!
	ti aéras/thíela!
All that rain/snow! _____	Τί βροχή/χιόνι!
	ti vrohí/hyóni!
All that fog! _____	Τί ομίχλη!
	ti omíchli!
How long has the _____ weather been like this here?	Από πότε κάνει τέτοιον καιρό εδώ; *apó póte káni tétyo keró edhó?*
Is it always this hot/cold ___ here?	Πάντα κάνει τόση ζέστη/τόσο κρύο εδώ; *pánda káni tósi zésti/tóso krío edhó?*
Is it always this dry/wet____ here?	Εχει πάντα εδώ τόση ξηρασία/υγρασία; *éhi pánda edhó tósi xirasía/ighrasía?*

3 .6 Hobbies

Do you have any _____ hobbies?	Εχετε χόμπυ; *éhete hóbi?*
I like painting/_____ reading/photography/	Μ' αρέσει να πλέκω/να διαβάζω/η φωτογραφία *marési na pléko/na dhiavázo/i fotoghrafía*
I like music _____	Αγαπώ τη μουσική *aghapó ti moosikí*
I like playing the _____ guitar/piano	Μ' αρέσει να παίζω κιθάρα/πιάνο *marési na pézo kithára/pyáno*
I like going to the _____ movies	Μ' αρέσει να πηγαίνω στον κινηματογράφο *marési na piyéno stonginimatoghráfo*
I like travelling/_____ sport/fishing/walking	Μ' αρέσει να ταξιδεύω/να κάνω σπορ/να ψαρεύω/να πηγαίνω περίπατο *marési na taxidhévo/na káno spor/na psarévo/na piyéno perípato*

3 .7 Being the host(ess)

See also 4 Eating out

Can I offer you a drink? ____	Μπορώ να σας προσφέρω ένα ποτό; *boró na sas prosféro éna potó?*
What would you like_____ to drink?	Τί θέλεις να πιεις; *ti thélis na pyis?*
Would you like a _____ cigarette/cigar/to roll your own?	Θέλετε ένα τσιγάρο/ένα πούρο/να στρίψετε ένα τσιγάρο; *thélete éna tsigháro/éna póoro/na strípsete éna tsigháro*
Something non-_____ alcoholic, please	Θα ήθελα ένα ποτό χωρίς αλκοόλ/ένα αναψυκτικό *tha íthela éna potó chorís alkól/éna anapsiktikó*
I don't smoke _____	Δεν καπνίζω *dhen kapnízo*

3 .8 Invitations

| Are you doing anything____ tonight? | Είσαι ελεύθερος/ελεύθερη απόψε; *íse eléftheros/eléftheri apópse?* |
| Do you have any plans ____ for today/this afternoon/tonight? | Εχετε κανένα πρόγραμμα για σήμερα/για το απόγευμα/για απόψε; *éhete kanéna próghrama ya símera/ya to apóyevma/ya apópse?* |

Would you like to go _____ out with me?	Θα θέλατε να βγούμε έξω μαζί; *tha thélate na vghóome éxo mazí?*
Would you like to go _____ dancing with me?	Θα θέλατε να πάμε να χορέψοομε μαζί; *tha thélate na páme na chorépsoome mazí?*
Would you like to have ____ lunch/dinner with me?	Θα θέλατε να πάμε να φάμε μαζί; *tha thélate na páme na fáme mazí?*
Would you like to come____ to the beach with me?	Θα θέλατε να πάμε μαζί στην παραλία; *tha thélate na páme mazí stimbaralía?*
Would you like to come____ into town with us?	Θα θέλατε να' ρθείτε μαζί μας στην πόλη; *tha thélate narthíte mazí mas stimbóli?*
Would you like to come____ and see some friends with us?	Θα θέλατε να' ρθείτε μαζί μας σε φίλους μας; *tha thélate narthíte mazí mas se fíloos mas?*
Shall we dance?_____	Πάμε να χορέψουμε; *páme na chorépsoome?*
– sit at the bar? _____	Πάμε να καθίσουμε στο μπαρ; *páme na kathísoome sto bar?*
– get something to drink? __	Πάμε να πιούμε κάτι; *páme na pyóome káti?*
– go for a walk/drive?_____	Πάμε να κάνουμε μια βόλτα/μια βόλτα με το αυτοκίνητο; *páme na kánoome mya vólta/mya vólta me to aftokínito*
Yes, all right _____	Ναι, εντάξει *ne, endáxi*
Good idea _____	Καλή ιδέα *kalí idhéa*
No (thank you) _____	Οχι, (ευχαριστώ) *óhi (efcharistó)*
Maybe later_____	Ισως αργότερα *ísos arghótera*
I don't feel like it _____	Δεν έχω όρεξη *dhen écho órexi*
I don't have time _____	Δεν έχω καιρό *dhen écho keró*
I already have a date _____	Εχω ένα άλλο ραντεβού *écho éna álo randevóo*
I'm not very good at_____ dancing/volleyball/ swimming	Δεν ξέρω να χορεύω/να παίζω βόλλευ/να κολυμπώ *dhen xéro na chorévo/na pézo vóllei/na kolimbó*

3 .9 Paying a compliment

You look wonderful! _____	Είστε μια χαρά! *íste mya chará!*
I like your car! _____	Τί ωραίο αυτοκίνητο! *ti oréo aftokínito!*
You're a nice boy/girl _____	Είσαι πολύ καλό παιδί/κορίτσι *íse polí kaló pedhí/korítsi*
What a sweet child! _____	Τί γλυκό παιδάκι! *ti ghlikó pedháki!*
You're a wonderful _____ dancer!	Χορεύετε πολύ καλά *chorévete polí kalá*
You're a wonderful _____ cook!	Μαγειρεύετε πολύ καλά *mayirévete polí kalá*
You're a terrific soccer ____ player!	Παίζετε πολύ καλά ποδόσφαιρο *pézete polí kalá podhósfero*

3

I like being with you _____	Μ' αρέσει να είμαι μαζί σου
	marési na íme mazí soo
I've missed you so much __	Μου έλειψες πολύ
	moo élipses polí
I dreamt about you _____	Σε είδα στ' όνειρό μου
	se ída stoniró moo
I think about you all day ___	Δε βγαίνεις από το νου μου
	dhe vyénis apó to noo moo
You have such a sweet _____ smile	Εχεις ένα γλυκό χαμόγελο
	éhis éna ghlikó chamóyelo
You have such beautiful ___ eyes	Εχεις πολύ ωραία μάτια
	éhis polí oréa mátya
I'm in love with you _____	Είμαι ερωτευμένος/ερωτευμένη μαζί σου
	íme erotevménos/erotevméni mazí soo
I'm in love with you too ___	Κι εγώ με σένα
	kyeghó me séna
I love you_____	Σ' αγαπώ
	saghapó
I love you too _____	Κι εγώ σ' αγαπώ
	kyeghó saghapó
I don't feel as strongly _____ about you	Εγώ δεν έχω τέτοια σοβαρά αισθήματα για σένα
	eghó dhen écho tétya sovará esthímata ya séna
I already have a _____ boyfriend/girlfriend	Εχω ήδη φίλο/φιλενάδα
	écho ídhi fílo/filenádha
I'm not ready for that_____	Δεν είμαι έτοιμος/έτοιμη γι' αυτό
	dhen íme étimos/étimi yaftó
This is going too fast _____ for me	Καλύτερα να μη βιαζόμαστε τόσο
	kalítera na mi viazómaste tóso
Take your hands off me____	Μη μ' αγγίζεις
	mi mangízis
Okay, no problem _____	Εντάξει, δεν πειράζει
	endáxi, dhembirázi
Will you stay with me _____ tonight?	Θα μείνεις μαζί μου τη νύχτα;
	tha mínis mazí moo ti níchta
I'd like to go to bed_____ with you	Θέλω να κάνουμε έρωτα
	thélo na kánoome érota
Only if we use a condom __	Μόνο με προφυλακτικό
	móno me profilaktikó
We have to be careful _____ about AIDS	Πρέπει να προσέχουμε λόγω του ΕΙΤΖ
	prépi na proséchoome lógho too AIDS
That's what they all say____	Ολοι τα ίδια λένε
	óli ta ídhya léne
We shouldn't take any _____ risks	Ας μη το διακινδυνέψουμε
	mi to dhiakindhinépsoome
Do you have a condom? ___	Εχεις προφυλακτικό;
	éhis profilaktikó?
No? In that case we _____ won't do it	Οχι; Τότε δε γίνεται
	óhi? tóte dhe yínete

3.11 Arrangements

When will I see you again?	Πότε θα σε ξαναδώ; *póte tha se xanadhó?*
Are you free over the weekend?	Θα έχετε καιρό το Σαββατοκύριακο; *tha éhete keró to savatokíriako?*
What shall we arrange?	Τί θα κανονίσουμε; *ti tha kanonísoome?*
Where shall we meet?	Πού θα συναντηθούμε; *poo tha sinandithóome?*
Will you pick me/us up?	Θα 'ρθείτε να με/μας πάρετε; *tharthíte na me/mas párete?*
Shall I pick you up?	Να περάσω να σας πάρω; *na peráso na sas páro?*
I have to be home by...	Πρέπει να είμαι σπίτι στις... *prépi na íme spíti stis...*
Can I take you home?	Μπορώ να σας πάω σπίτι; *boró na sas páo spíti?*
I don't want to see you anymore	Δε θέλω να σας ξαναδώ *dhe thélo na sas xanadhó*

3.12 Saying goodbye

Can I write/call you?	Μπορώ να σας γράψω/τηλεφωνήσω; *boró na sas ghrápso/tilefoníso?*
Will you write/call me?	Θα μου γράψετε/τηλεφωνήσετε; *tha moo ghrápsete/tilefonísete?*
Can I have your address/phone number?	Μπορώ να έχω τη διεύθυνσή σας/τον αριθμό του τηλεφώνου σας; *boró na écho ti dhiéfihinsi sas/ton arithmó too tilefónoo sas?*
Thanks for everything	Ευχαριστώ για όλα *efcharistó ya óla*
It was very nice	Ήταν πολύ ωραία *ítan polí oréa*
Say hello to...	Χαιρετισμούς σε... *heretizmóos se...*
All the best	Σου εύχομαι ό,τι καλύτερο *soo éfchome óti kalítero*
Good luck	Καλή επιτυχία στο μέλλον *kalí epitihía sto mélon*
When will you be back?	Πότε θα ξαναέρθεις; *póte tha xanaérthis?*
I'll be waiting for you	Θα σε περιμένω *tha se periméno*
I'd like to see you again	Θα ήθελα πολύ να σε ξαναδώ *tha íthela polí na se xanadhó*
I hope we meet again soon	Ελπίζω να ξαναιδωθούμε σύντομα *elpízo na xanaidhothóome síndoma*
This is our address. If you're ever in the UK...	Αυτή είναι η διεύθυνσή μας. Αν κάποτε βρεθείτε στο Ηνωμένο Βασίλειο... *aftí íne i dhiéfthinsí mas. an kápote vrethíte sto inoméno vasílio...*
You'd be more than welcome	Είστε πάντα ευπρόσδεκτος/ευπρόσδεκτη *íste pánda efprósdhektos/efprósdhekti*

Eating out

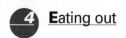

4 Eating out

● **In Greece** people usually have three meals:
1 *το πρωινό* (breakfast), between 7.00 and 10 am. Breakfast is light and consists of a cup of coffee with bread and jam or honey.
2 *το γεύμα* (lunch), between 1.00 and 3.00pm. Lunch always includes a hot dish and is the most important meal of the day.
3 *το δείπνο* (dinner), between 9.00pm and 1.00am. Dinner is a hot meal similar to lunch though a little lighter. It is usually taken with the family.

4 .1 On arrival

I'd like to book a table _____ for seven o'clock, please	Μπορώ να κλείσω ένα τραπέζι γι' απόψε στις εφτά; *boró na klíso éna trapézi yapópse stis eftá?*
I'd like a table for two, _____ please	Θα ήθελα ένα τραπέζι για δύο άτομα *tha íthela éna trapézi ya dhío átoma*
We've/we haven't booked __	(Δεν) κλείσαμε τραπέζι *(dhen) klísame trapézi*
Is the restaurant open _____ yet?	Είναι ανοιχτή η κουζίνα; *íne anichtí i koozína?*
What time does the _____ restaurant open/close?	Πότε ανοίγει/κλείνει η κουζίνα; *póte aníyi/klíni i koozína?*
Can we wait for a table? ___	Μπορούμε να περιμένουμε για ένα τραπέζι; *boróome na periménoome ya éna trapézi?*
Will we have to _____ wait long?	Θα πρέπει να περιμένουμε πολλή ώρα; *tha prépi na periménoome polí óra?*
Is this seat taken? _____	Είναι ελεύθερη αυτή η θέση; *íne eléftheri aftí i thési?*
Could we sit here/there? ___	Μπορούμε να καθίσουμε εδώ/εκεί; *boróome na kathísoome edhó/ekí?*
Can we sit by the_____ window?	Μπορούμε να καθίσουμε κοντά στο παράθυρο; *boróome na kathísoome kondá sto paráthiro?*
Can we eat outside? _____	Μπορούμε να φάμε κι έξω; *boróome na fáme kyéxo?*
Do you have another _____ chair for us?	Μας φέρνετε ακόμα μια καρέκλα; *mas férnete akóma mya karékla?*
Do you have a highchair? __	Μας φέρνετε μια παιδική καρέκλα; *mas férnete mya pedhikí karékla?*
Is there a socket for _____ this bottle-warmer?	Υπάρχει μια πρίζα γι' αυτό το βραστήρα; *ipárhi mya príza yaftó to vrastíra?*

Κλείσατε τραπέζι; _____	Do you have a reservation?
Με ποιό όνομα;_____	What name, please?
Από δω, παρακαλώ	This way, please
Αυτό το τραπέζι είναι κλεισμένο_____	This table is reserved
Σ' ένα τέταρτο θά 'χουμε ελεύθερο _____ τραπέζι	We'll have a table free in fifteen minutes
Μπορείτε να περιμένετε στο (μπαρ); ___	Would you like to wait (at the bar)?

Could you warm up _____ this bottle/jar for me?	Μπορείτε να μου ζεστάνετε αυτό το μπιμπερό/βαζάκι;
	boríte na moo zestánete avtó to biberó/vazáki?
Not too hot, please _____	Να μην είναι πολύ ζεστό, παρακαλώ
	na min íne polí zestó, parakaló
Is there somewhere I _____ can change the baby's nappy?	Υπάρχει κάποιος χώρος όπου μπορώ να αλλάξω το μωρό;
	ipárhi kápyos chóros ópoo boró na aláxo to moró?
Where are the toilets? _____	Πού είναι η τουαλέτα;
	poo íne i twaléta?

 .2 Ordering

Waiter!/Madam!/Sir!_____	Γκαρσόνι!/Κυρία!/Κύριε!
	garsóni!/kiría!/kírie!
We'd like something to _____ eat/a drink	Θέλουμε να φάμε/να πιούμε κάτι
	théloome na fáme/na pyóome káti
Could I have a quick_____ meal?	Μπορώ να φάω κάτι γρήγορα;
	boró na fáo káti ghrígora?
We don't have much _____ time	Βιαζόμαστε
	viazómaste
We'd like to have a _____ drink first	Θέλουμε πρώτα να πιούμε κάτι
	théloome próta na pyóome káti
Could we see the_____ menu/wine list, please?	Μπορούμε να δούμε τον κατάλογο/τον κατάλογο κρασιών;
	boróome na dhóome tongatálogho/tongatálogho krasyón?
Do you have a menu _____ in English?	Εχετε ένα κατάλογο στα αγγλικά;
	éhete éna katálogho sta angliká?
Do you have a dish_____ of the day?/Do you have a tourist menu?	Εχετε πιάτο της ημέρας/τουριστικό μενού;
	éhete pyáto tis iméras/tooristikó menóo?
We haven't made a _____ choice yet	Δεν αποφασίσαμε ακόμα
	dhen apofasísame akóma
What do you_____ recommend?	Τί μπορείτε να μας προτείνετε;
	ti boríte na mas protínete?
What are the specialities_____ of the region/the house?	Ποιές είναι οι σπεσιαλιτέ της περιοχής/του μαγαζιού;
	pyes íne i spesialité tis periohís/too maghazyóo?
I like strawberries/olives _____	Μ' αρέσουν οι φράουλες/οι ελιές
	marésoon i fráooles/i elyés
I don't like fish/meat... _____	Δε μ' αρέσει το ψάρι/το κρέας/...
	dhe marési to psári/to kréas/...
What's this?_____	Τί είναι αυτό;
	ti íne aftó?
Does it have...in it? _____	Εχει μέσα...;
	éhi mésa...?
What does it taste like? _____	Με τί μοιάζει;
	me ti myázi?
Is this a hot or a_____ cold dish?	Αυτό το φαγητό είναι κρύο ή ζεστό;
	aftó to fayitó íne krío i zestó?
Is this sweet? _____	Αυτό το φαγητό είναι γλυκό;
	aftó to fayitó íne ghlikó?

Eating out

Is this spicy/hot? _____ Αυτό το φαγητό είναι πικάντικο/πιπεράτο;
aftó to fayitó íne pikándiko/piperáto?

Do you have _____ Μήπως έχετε κάτι άλλο;
anything else? *mípos éhete káti álo?*

I'm on a salt-free diet _____ Απαγορεύεται να τρώω αλάτι
apaghorévete na tró-o aláti

I can't eat pork _____ Απαγορεύεται να τρώω χοιρινό κρέας
apaghorévete na tró-o hirinó kréas

– sugar _____ Απαγορεύεται να τρώω ζάχαρη
apaghorévete na tró-o záchari

– fatty foods _____ Απαγορεύεται να τρώω λίπη
apaghorévete na tró-o lípi

– (hot) spices _____ Απαγορεύεται να τρώω (καυτερά)
μπαχαρικά
apaghorévete na tró-o (kafterá) bachariká

I'll/we'll have what those___ Θέλουμε το ίδιο φαγητό που τρώνε
people are having εκείνοι οι άνθρωποι, παρακαλώ
théloome to ídhyo fayitó poo tróne ekíni i ánthropi, parakaló

I'd like... _____ Θα ήθελα...
tha íthela ...

We're not having a _____ Δε θέλουμε ορεκτικό
starter *dhe théloome orektikó*

The child will share what __ Το παιδί θα φάει λίγο από το δικό μας
we're having φαγητό
to pedhí tha fái lígho apó to dhikó mas fayitó

Could I have some _____ Παρακαλώ, λίγο ψωμί ακόμα
more bread, please? *parakaló, lígho psomí akóma*

– a bottle of water/wine____ Παρακαλώ, ένα μπουκάλι νερό/κρασί
ακόμα
parakaló, éna bookáli neró/krasí akóma

– another helping of... _____ Παρακαλώ, μια μερίδα... ακόμα
parakaló, mya merídha ... akóma

– some salt and pepper _____ Μας φέρνετε το αλατοπίπερο, παρακαλώ;
mas férnete to alatopípero, parakaló?

– a napkin _____ Μας φέρνετε μια χαρτοπετσέτα,
παρακαλώ;
mas férnete mya chartopetséta, parakaló

– a spoon _____ Μας φέρνετε ένα κουταλάκι, παρακαλώ;
mas férnete éna kootaláki, parakaló?

– an ashtray _____ Μας φέρνετε ένα τασάκι, παρακαλώ;
mas férnete éna tasáki, parakaló?

– some matches _____ Μας φέρνετε σπίρτα, παρακαλώ;
mas férnete spírta, parakaló?

– some toothpicks _____ Μας φέρνετε οδοντογλυφίδες,
παρακαλώ;
mas férnete odhondoghlifídhes, parakaló?

– a glass of water _____ Μας φέρνετε ένα ποτήρι νερό, παρακαλώ;
mas férnete éna potíri neró, parakaló?

– a straw (for the child) ____ Μας φέρνετε ένα καλαμάκι (για το παιδί),
παρακαλώ;
mas férnete éna kalamáki (ya to pédhi), parakaló?

Enjoy your meal! _____ Καλή όρεξη!
kalí órexi!

Θέλετε να φάτε; _____	Do you want to eat?
Διαλέξατε τί θέλετε να φάτε; _____	Have you decided what you want?
Θέλετε ένα απεριτίφ; _____	Would you like a drink first?
Τί θέλετε να πιείτε; _____	What would you like to drink?
Καλή όρεξη _____	Enjoy your meal
Θέλετε ένα γλυκό/ένα καφέ; _____	Would you like a dessert/coffee?

You too! _____	Επίσης
	epísis
Cheers! _____	Στην υγειά σας!
	stin iyá sas!
The next round's on me ___	Το επόμενο κέρασμα είναι δικό μου
	to epómeno kyérazma íne dhikó moo
Could we have a doggy _____ bag, please?	Μπορούμε να πάρουμε τ' απομεινάρια για το σκύλο μας;
	boróome na pároome tapominária ya to skílo mas?

4 .3 The bill

See also 8.2 Settling the bill

How much is this dish? _____	Πόσο κάνει αυτό το φαγητό;
	póso káni aftó to fayitó?
Could I have the bill, _____ please?	Το λογαριασμό, παρακαλώ
	to loghariazmó, parakaló
All together _____	Ολα μαζί
	óla mazí
Everyone pays separately ___	Ο καθένας πληρώνει τα δικά του
	o kathénas pliróni ta dhiká too
Could we have the menu ___ again, please?	Μπορούμε να ξαναδούμε τον κατάλογο;
	boróome na xanadhóome tongatálogho?
The...is not on the bill _____	Το...δεν είναι στο λογαριασμό
	to...dhen íne sto loghariazmó

4 .4 Complaints

It's taking a very _____ long time	Αργείτε πολύ
	aryíte polí
We've been here an _____ hour already	Περιμένουμε ήδη μια ώρα
	periménoome ídhi mya óra
This must be a mistake ____	Πρέπει να έγινε κάποιο λάθος
	prépi na éyine kápyo láthos
This is not what I _____ ordered	Δεν παράγγειλα αυτό
	dhen parángila aftó
I ordered... _____	Παράγγειλα...
	parángila...
There's a dish missing _____	Λείπει ένα φαγητό
	lípi éna fayitó

This is broken/not clean ___	Αυτό είναι σπασμένο/δεν είναι καθαρό
	aftó íne spazméno/dhen íne katharó
The food's cold _____	Το φαγητό είναι κρύο
	to fayitó íne krío
– not fresh _____	Το φαγητό δεν είναι φρέσκο
	to fayitó dhen íne frésko
– too salty/sweet/spicy ____	Το φαγητό είναι πολύ αλμυρό/γλυκό/πικάντικο
	to fayitó íne polí almiró/ghlikó/pikándiko
The meat's not done_____	Το κρέας δεν είναι ψημένο
	to kréas dhen íne psiméno
– overdone _____	Το κρέας είναι πολύ ψημένο
	to kréas íne polí psiméno
– tough _____	Το κρέας είναι σκληρό
	to kréas íne skliró
– off_____	Το κρέας είναι χαλασμένο
	to kréas íne chalazméno
Could I have something ___ else instead of this?	Μπορείτε να μου δώσετε κάτι άλλο;
	boríte na moo dhósete káti álo?
The bill/this amount is ____ not right	Ο λογαριασμός/αυτό το ποσό δεν είναι σωστός/σωστό
	o loghariazmós/aftó to posó dhen íne sostós/sostó
We didn't have this_____	Αυτό δεν το είχαμε
	aftó dhen to íchame
There's no paper in the ___ toilet	Δεν έχει χαρτί στην τουαλέτα
	dhen éhi chartí stin twaléta
Do you have a _____ complaints book?	Εχετε βιβλίο παραπόνων;
	éhete vivlío parapónon?
Will you call the_____ manager, please?	Φωνάξτε το αφεντικό σας, παρακαλώ
	fonáxte to afendikósas, parakaló

4 .5 Paying a compliment

That was a wonderful _____ meal	Φάγαμε πολύ καλά
	fághame polí kalá
The food was excellent ____	Ηταν πολύ νόστιμο
	ítan polí nóstimo
The...in particular was _____ delicious	Προπαντός το...ήταν εξαιρετικό
	propandós to...ítan exeretikó

αλκοολούχα ποτά alcoholic beverages	λαχανικά vegetables	σούπες soups
απεριτίφ aperitif	μεζέδες mixed starters (also	σπεσιαλιτέ speciality
επιδόρπια dessert	used when drinking ouzo)	συμπεριλαμβανομένης υπηρεσίας
ζεστά φαγητά hot dishes	ντόπια φαγητά local dishes	service included της σχάρας
θαλασσινά seafood	ορεκτικά appetisers	grilled dishes της ώρας
κατά προτίμηση prepared as you want it	πάστες cakes/pastries	prepared while you wait Φ.Π.Α.
κατάλογος κρασιών wine list	πιάτα της ημέρας dish of the day	VAT φαγητά για
κρέας meat	πουλερικά poultry	χορτοφάγους vegetarian dishes
κρύα φαγητά cold dishes	πρωινό breakfast	ψάρι fish

4.7 Alphabetical list of drinks and dishes

αγγούρι cucumber	βερύκοκα apricots	γίγαντες large white beans
αγκινάρες globe artichokes	βοδινό κρέας beef	γιουβαρλάκια meatballs
αλάτι salt	βούτυρο butter	γιουβέτσι a form of pasta
αμύγδαλο (-λα) almond (s)	βραστό boiled	γλώσσα sole (fish)
αντίδια endives	βυσσινάδα sour cherry	γραβιέρα cheese
αντσούγιες anchovies	drink γάλα	γρανίτα a drink made
αρακάς peas	milk γαλακτομπούρεκο	with crushed ice and fruit
αρνί/αρνίσιο κρέα lamb	cake made with filo pastry	δαμάσκηνο (-να) plums/prunes
αστακός lobster	and confectioner's custard	δάφνη bayleaf
αυγά μάτι fried eggs	γαλλόπουλο turkey	ελιές olives
αυγολέμονο egg and lemon	γαρίδες prawns	ζαμπόν ham
(sauce or soup) αχλάδι(α)	γεμιστό stuffed	ζάχαρη sugar
pear(s) βασιλόπιτα	γιαούρτι yoghurt	ζουμί broth
New Year's cake βατόμουρα	γιαχνί a stew	θυμάρι thyme
blackberries		

ιμάμ-μπαϊλντί
a dish of aubergines baked with tomato and garlic

καβούρι
crab

κακαβιά
a fish soup

καλαμαράκι
squid

καλαμπόκι
corn on the cob

καραβίδα
crayfish

καραμέλλα
a boiled sweet

καρότα
carrots

καρπούζι
water melon

καρύδια
walnuts

κασέρι
hard parmesan-like cheese

κάστανο
chestnut

καταΐφι
a cake made with honey, and nuts

κατσικάκι
kid

καφές
coffee

καφές φραπέ
iced coffee

κεράσι (α)
cherry (cherries)

κεφαλοτύρι
hard cheese

κεφτέδες
fried meatballs

κιμάς
minced meat

κίτρο
lime

κοκκινιστό
baked in a tomato sauce

κοκορέτσι
tripe cooked on a skewer

κολοκυθάκι
courgettes

κολοκύθι
marrow/pumpkin

κομπόστα
compote

κοτόπουλο
chicken

κουκιά
broad beans

κουλουράκι (α)
small ring-shaped biscuits

κουλούρι
hard ring-shaped sesame bread

κουνέλι
rabbit

κουραμπιέδες
cakes made with almonds and caster sugar

κρασί
wine

κρέας
meat

κρέμα
confectioner's custard

κρεμμύδι(α)
onion(s)

κυνήγι
game

λαγός
hare

λάδι
oil

λαχανάκια Βρυξελλών
Brussels sprouts

λαχανικό (-κά)
vegetable(s)

λάχανο
cabbage

λεμονάδα
lemonade

λεμόνι
lemon

λουκάνικα
sausages

λουκουμάδες
light doughnuts served with spiced honey

λουκούμι
Turkish Delight

μαγειρίτσα
an Easter soup made from lamb and goat entrails

μαϊντανό
parsley

μανιτάρι
mushrooms

μανούρι
a white cheese

μαρίδες
whitebait

μαρμελάδα
jam

μαρούλι
lettuce

μέλι
honey

μελιτζάνα
aubergine

μελομακάρονα
cakes made of honey and nuts

μήλο
apple

μιζήθρα
a soft goat's cheese

μοσχάρι/μοσχαρίσιο κρέας
veal

μοσχοκάρυδο
nutmeg

μούρο
mulberry

μουσακάς
a dish made with layers of minced lamb and aubergine

μούσμουλα
loquat

μουστάρδα
mustard

μπακαλιάρος
dried cod

μπακλαβάς
cake made with filo pastry, nuts and honey

μπάμιες
okra

μπαρμπούνι
red mullet

μπιζέλια
peas

μπιφτέκι
burger

μπουγάτσα
a cake made with filo pastry and confectioner's custard

μπούτι
thigh

μπριζόλα βοδινή
beef chop/cutlet

μπύρα
beer

μυαλά
brains

μύδια
mussels

νερό
water

νεφρά
kidneys

ντολμάδες
stuffed vine-leaves

ντομάτες
tomatoes

ντομάτες γεμιστές
stuffed tomatoes

ξηροί καρποί
dried fruit

ξίδι/ξύδι
vinegar

ομελέτα
omelette

ούζο
ouzo (aniseed-flavoured spirit)

ουίσκυ
whiskey

παγωτό
ice cream

παϊδάκι
lamb chop

παντζάρια
beetroots

πάπια
duck

παπουτσάκια
stuffed aubergines

πάστες
cakes

παστίτσιο
minced meat and macaroni pie

παστό
salted

πατάτες
potatoes

πατσάς
soup made from tripe

πεπόνι
melon

πέστροφα
trout

πετεινάρι κρασάτο
coq au vin

πιλάφι
pilaff rice

πιπέρι
pepper

πιπεριά
green or red pepper (vegetable)

πιτσούνι
young pigeons

πλάτη
shoulder

πορτοκαλάδα
orange juice/orangeade

πορτοκάλι
orange

πράσο
leek

ραδίκια
chicory

ραπανάκια
radishes

ρεβύθια
chick-peas

ρέγγα
herring (smoked)

ρετσίνα
wine flavoured with pine resin

ρίγανη
oregano

ροδάκινο
peach

ρόδι
pomegranate

ρύζι
rice

ρυζόγαλο
rice pudding

σαλάτα
salad

σαλιγγάρια
snails

σάλτσα
sauce

σαντιγί
whipped cream

σάντουιτς
sandwich

σαρδέλλες
sardines

σέλινο
celery

σκορδαλιά
dip made from garlic and bread or potato

σκόρδο
garlic

σκουμπρί
mackerel

σοκολάτα
chocolate

σολομός
salmon

σουβλάκι
grilled meat on a skewer

σούπα
soup

σουπιές
cuttle fish

σουτζουκάκια
spicy meat-balls in tomato sauce

σπανάκι
spinach

στα κάρβουνα
barbecued

σταφίδα
raisin

σταφύλια
grapes

στη σχάρα
on the grill

στιφάδο
stew made with shallots and flavoured with sweet wine

στο φούρνο
cooked in the oven

στρείδι
oysters

σύκα
figs

συκώτι
liver

σφυρίδα
grey mullet

ταραμάς
smoked cod's roe

ταραμοσαλάτα
paste made from
  smoked cod's roe
τασκεμπάμπ
shishkebab
τζατζίκι
cucumber and
  yoghurt dip
τηγανίτα
fritter
τηγανιτό
fried
τόννος
tuna
τούρτα
gateau, layer-cake
τσάι
tea
τσίχλες/μαστίχι
chewing gum
τσικουδιά
a sort of spirit
τσίπουρο
a sort of spirit
τσουρέκι
Easter loaf
τυρί
cheese
Τυρόπιτα
cheese pie

φασκόμηλο
aromatic herb tea
φασολάκια
green beans
φασόλια
haricot beans
φέτα
goat's cheese
φιλέτο
fillet steak
φουντούκια
hazelnuts
φράουλες
strawberries
φράπα
a variety of grapefruit
φρούτο
fruit
φρυγανιά
toast, French-style
φυστίκια
pistachio nuts
χαβιάρι
caviar
χαλβάς
a sweet made with
  semolina, honey
  and nuts
χαμομήλι
camomile

χέλι
eel
χήνα
goose
χοιρινό
pork
χόρτα
green dandelion
  leaves used in
  salad
χουρμάς
date
χταπόδι
octopus
χυμός
juice
χωριάτικη σαλάτα
a salad made
from tomatoes,
  cucumber, black
  olives and goat's
  cheese
ψάρι
fish
ψητό
roast/baked
ψωμί
bread

On the road

5 On the road

5.1 Asking for directions

English	Greek	Transliteration
Excuse me, could I ask you something?	Συγγνώμη, μπορώ να σας ρωτήσω κάτι;	sighnómi, boró na sas rotíso káti?
I've lost my way	'Εχασα το δρόμο	échasa to dhrómo
Is there a(n)... around here?	Ξέρετε κανένα...εδώ κοντά;	xérete kanéna...edhó kondá?
Is this the way to...?	Αυτός είναι ο δρόμος για..;	aftós íne o dhrómos ya...?
Could you tell me how to get to... (name of place)	Μπορείτε να μου πείτε πώς μπορώ να πάω σε... ;	boríte na moo píte pos boró na páo se...?
What's the quickest way to...?	Ποιός είναι ο πιο σύντομος δρόμος για... ;	pyos íne o pyo síndomos dhrómos ya ...?
How many kilometres is it to...?	Πόσα χιλιόμετρα είναι ακόμα ως...;	pósa hilyómetra íne akóma os...?
Could you point it out on the map?	Μπορείτε να το δείξετε στο χάρτη;	boríte na to dhíxete sto chartí?

Δεν ξέρω, δεν είμαι από δω	I don't know, I don't know my way around here
Πήρατε λάθος δρόμο	You're going the wrong way
Πρέπει να γυρίσετε σε...	You have to go back to...
Εκεί θ' ακολουθήσετε τις πινακίδες	From there on just follow the signs
Εκεί θα ξαναρωτήσετε	When you get there, ask again

ίσια	straight ahead
αριστερά	left
δεξιά	right
στρίβω	turn
ακολουθώ	follow
περνάω το δρόμο	cross the road
η διασταύρωση	the intersection
ο δρόμος/η οδός	the street
το φανάρι	the traffic light
το τούνελ	the tunnel
η πινακίδα διασταύρωση προτεραιότητας	the `give way' sign
το κτίριο	the building
στη γωνιά	at the corner
το ποτάμι	the river
η ανισόπεδη διασταύρωση	the flyover
η γέφυρα	the bridge
η διάβαση του τρένου/οι μπάρες	the level crossing
η πινακίδα που δείχνει το δρόμο για...	the sign pointing to...
το βέλος	the arrow

● **Border documents:** valid passport. For car and motorbike: valid UK driving licence and registration document, insurance document, green card, UK registration plate. Caravan: must be entered on the green card and driven with the same registration number. A warning triangle, headlamp converters and extra headlamp bulbs should be carried. Insurance should also be upgraded.

Import and export specifications:

Foreign currency: a maximum of 100,000 drachmas may be taken into the country, and a maximum of 20,000 may be taken out.

Alcohol (aged 18 and above): 1 and a half litres of spirits, fortified or sparkling wine. Tobacco (aged 17 and above): 300 cigarettes or 150 cigars or 400 grams of tobacco.

Το διαβατήριό σας, παρακαλώ _____	Your passport, please
Την πράσινη κάρτα σας, παρακαλώ _____	Your green card, please
Τον αριθμό κυκλοφορίας σας, _____ παρακαλώ	Your vehicle documents, please
Τη βίζα σας, παρακαλώ_____	Your visa, please
Πού πάτε:_____	Where are you heading?
Πόσο καιρό σκοπεύετε να μείνετε; _____	How long are you planning to stay?
Έχετε τίποτα να δηλώσετε; _____	Do you have anything to declare?
Ανοίξτε αυτό, παρακαλώ _____	Open this, please

My children are entered ___ on this passport	Τα παιδιά μου είναι γραμμένα σ' αυτό το διαβατήριο _ta pedhyámoo íne ghraména saftó to dhiavatírio_
I'm travelling through _____	Είμαι περαστικός/περαστική _íme perastikós/perastikí_
I'm going on holiday to... _	Πηγαίνω για διακοπές σε... _piyéno ya dhiakopés se_
I'm on a business trip _____	Είμαι εδώ για δουλειές _íme edhó ya dhoolyés_
I don't know how long_____ I'll be staying yet	Δεν ξέρω ακόμα πόσο καιρό θα μείνω _dhengxéro akóma póso kyeró tha míno_
I'll be staying here for _____ a weekend	Θα μείνω εδώ ένα Σαββατοκύριακο _tha míno edhó éna savatokíryako_
– for a few days _____	Θα μείνω εδώ λίγες μέρες _tha míno edhó líyes méres_
– for a week_____	Θα μείνω εδώ μία εβδομάδα _tha míno edhó mía evdhomádha_
– for two weeks _____	Θα μείνω εδώ δύο εβδομάδες _tha míno edhó dhío evdhomádhes_
I've got nothing to_____ declare	Δεν έχω τίποτα να δηλώσω _dhenécho típota na dhilóso_
I've got...with me_____	Έχω...μαζί μου _écho...mazímoo_

On the road

– ...cartons of cigarettes ___	Έχω μία κούτα τσιγάρα μαζί μου
	écho mía kóota tsighára mazímoo
– a bottle of... ___	Έχω ένα μπουκάλι... μαζί μου
	écho éna bookáli...mazímoo
– some souvenirs ___	Έχω μερικά σουβενίρ μαζί μου
	écho meriká soovenír mazímoo
These are personal ___ effects	Αυτά είναι προσωπικά αντικείμενα
	aftá íne prosopiká andikímena
These are not new ___	Αυτά τα πράματα δεν είναι καινούρια
	aftá ta prámata dhen íne kenóorya
Here's the receipt ___	Εδώ είναι η απόδειξη
	edhó íne i apódhixi
This is for private use ___	Αυτό είναι για προσωπική χρήση
	aftó íne ya prosopikí chrísi
How much import duty ___ do I have to pay?	Πόσο φόρο πρέπει να πληρώσω;
	póso fóro prépi na pliróso?
Can I go now? ___	Μπορώ να φύγω τώρα;
	boró na fígho tóra?

5 .3 Luggage

Porter! ___	Αχθοφόρε!
	achthofóre!
Could you take this ___ luggage to...?	Παρακαλώ, πηγαίνετε αυτές τις αποσκευές σε...
	parakaló, piyénete aftés tis aposkevés se...
How much do I ___ owe you?	Πόσο σας οφείλω;
	póso sas ofílo?
Where can I find a ___ luggage trolley?	Πού μπορώ να βρω ένα καροτσάκι;
	poo boró na vro éna karotsáki?
Could you store this ___ luggage for me?	Μπορώ να δώσω αυτές τις αποσκευές προς φύλαξη;
	boró na dhóso aftés tis aposkevés pros fílaxi?
Where are the luggage ___ lockers?	Που βρίσκονται οι θυρίδες αποσκευών;
	poo vrískonde i thirídhes aposkevón?
I can't get the locker ___ open	Δεν μπορώ να ανοίξω τη θυρίδα
	dhemboró na aníxo ti thirídha
How much is it per item ___ per day?	Πόσο κοστίζει το κομμάτι/ τη μέρα;
	póso kostízi to komáti/ti méra?
This is not my bag/ ___ suitcase	Αυτή δεν είναι δική μου τσάντα/βαλίτσα
	aftí dhen íne dhikímoo tsánda/valítsa
There's one item/bag/ ___ suitcase missing still	Λείπει ακόμα ένα κομμάτι/μια τσάντα/μια βαλίτσα
	lípi akóma éna komáti/mya tsánda/mya valítsa
My suitcase is damaged ___	Η βαλίτσα μου έπαθε κάποια ζημιά
	i valítsa moo épathe kápya zimyá

ΑΠΑΓΟΡΕΥΕΤΑΙ Η
ΠΡΟΣΠΕΡΑΣΗ
no overtaking

ΑΠΑΓΟΡΕΥΕΤΑΙ Η
ΣΤΑΘΜΕΥΣΗ
no parking

ΑΡΓΑ
slow

ΑΥΤΟΚΙΝΗΤΟΔΡΟΜΟΣ
road suitable for cars

ΑΦΥΛΑΚΤΗ
ΔΙΑΒΑΣΗ
unmanned crossing

ΔΕΥΤΕΡΕΥΩΝ
ΔΡΟΜΟΣ
minor road

ΔΙΑΧΩΡΙΣΜΟΣ
road divides

ΔΙΟΔΙΑ
toll

ΔΩΣΕΤΕ
ΠΡΟΤΕΡΑΙΟΤΗΤΑ
give way

ΕΘΝΙΚΗ ΟΔΟΣ
(ΜΕ ΔΙΟΔΙΑ)
motorway
(with toll)

ΕΙΣΟΔΟΣ
entrance

ΕΛΑΤΤΩΣΑΤΕ
ΤΑΧΥΤΗΤΑ
reduce speed

ΕΛΕΥΘΕΡΗ
ΚΥΚΛΟΦΟΡΙΑ
clearway

ΕΠΑΡΧΙΑΚΗ ΟΔΟΣ
minor road

ΕΠΙΚΙΝΔΥΝΗ
ΔΙΑΣΤΑΥΡΩΣΗ
dangerous junction

ΕΠΙΚΙΝΔΥΝΗ
ΚΑΤΩΦΕΡΕΙΑ
steep hill

ΕΠΙΚΙΝΔΥΝΗ
ΣΤΡΟΦΗ
dangerous bend

ΕΞΟΔΟΣ
exit

ΕΞΟΔΟΣ
ΟΧΗΜΑΤΩΝ
exit for heavy
goods vehicles

Η ΤΑΧΥΤΗΤΑ
ΕΛΕΓΧΕΤΑΙ ΜΕ
ΡΑΝΤΑΡ
radar speed checks

ΚΑΤΟΛΙΣΘΗΣΕΙΣ
loose chippings

ΚΕΝΤΡΟ
centre

ΚΙΝΔΥΝΟΣ
danger

ΚΛΕΙΣΤΗ ΟΔΟΣ
road closed

ΚΥΚΛΟΦΟΡΙΑ ΑΠΟ
ΑΝΤΙΘΕΤΗ
ΚΑΤΕΥΘΥΝΣΗ
oncoming traffic

ΜΟΝΟΔΡΟΜΟΣ
one-way street

ΝΟΣΟΚΟΜΕΙΟ
hospital

ΟΔΟΣ
ΠΡΟΤΕΡΑΙΟΤΗΤΑΣ
road with priority
over vehicles
entering from side
roads

ΠΑΡΑΚΑΜΠΤΗΡΙΟΣ
diversion

ΠΕΖΟΔΡΟΜΟΣ
pavement

ΠΕΡΙΜΕΝΕΤΕ
wait

ΠΡΟΣΟΧΗ
look out!

ΠΡΟΣ ΠΑΡΑΛΙΑ
to the beach

ΣΤΑΘΜΟΣ ΠΡΩΤΩΝ
ΒΟΗΘΕΙΩΝ
first aid post

ΣΤΕΝΩΜΑ
ΟΔΟΣΤΡΩΜΑΤΟΣ
road narrows

ΣΤΡΟΦΕΣ
bends

ΤΕΛΟΣ
ΑΠΑΓΟΡΕΥΜΕΝΗΣ
ΖΩΝΗΣ
end of forbidden
zone

ΥΨΟΣ
ΠΕΡΙΟΡΙΣΜΕΝΟ
restricted height

ΧΩΜΑΤΟΔΡΟΜΟΣ
packed-earth road

The parts of a car

(the diagram shows the numbered parts)

1	battery	η μπαταρία	i bataría
2	rear light	το πίσω φως	to píso fos
3	rear-view mirror	ο καθρέφτης οδηγήσεως	o kathréftis odhiyíseos
	reversing light	το πίσω φανάρι πορείας	to píso fanári porías
4	aerial	η αντένα	i anténa
	car radio	το ραδιόφωνο του αυτοκινήτου	to radhiófono too aftokinítoo
5	petrol tank	το ρεζερβουάρ	to rezervvár
6	sparking plugs	το μπουζί	to boozí
	fuel filter	το φίλτρο καυσίμων	to fíltro kafsímon
	fuel pump	η αντλία καυσίμων	i andlía kafsímon
7	wing mirror	ο εξωτερικός καθρέφτης	o exoterikós kathréftis
8	bumper	ο προφυλακτήρας	o profilaktíras
	carburettor	το καρμπυρατέρ	to karbiratér
	crankcase	το κάρτερ	to kárter
	cylinder	ο κύλινδρος	o kílindhros
	ignition	οι πλατίνες	i platínes
	warning light	η λάμπα ελέγχου	i lámpa elénchoo (to)
	dynamo	το δυναμό	to dhinamó
	accelerator	το πηδάλι γκάζι	to pidháli gaz i
	handbrake	το χειρόφρενο	to hirófreno
	valve	η βαλβίδα	i valvídha
9	silencer	ο σιγαστείρας	o sighastíras
10	boot	το πορτμπαγκάζ	to portbagáz
11	headlight	ο προβολέας	o provoléas
	crank shaft	ο στροφαλοφόρος	o strofalofóros
12	air filter	το φίλτρο αέρος	to fíltro aéros
	fog lamp	το πίσω φως ομίχλης	to píso fos omíchlis
13	engine block	το σώμα της μηχανής	to sóma tis mihanís
	camshaft	ο εκκεντροφόρος άξονας	o ekendrofóros áxonas
	oil filter	το φίλτρο λαδιού	to fíltro ladhyóo
	oil pump	η αντλία λαδιού	i andlía ladhyóo
	dipstick	ο δείκτης λαδιού	o dhíktis ladhyóo
	pedal	το πηδάλι	to pidháli
14	door	η πόρτα	i pórta
15	radiator	το ψυγείο	to psiyío
16	brake disc	ο δίσκος του φρένου	o dhiskos too frénoo
	spare wheel	η ρεσέρβα	i resérva
17	indicator	το φλας	to flas
18	windscreen wiper	ο γυαλοκαθαριστήρας	o yalokatharistíras
19	shock absorbers	τα αμορτισέρ	ta amortisér
	sunroof	η κινητή σκεπή	i kinití skepí
	starter motor	το στάρτερ	to stárter
20	steering column	η στήλη του τιμονιού	i stíli too timonyóo
21	exhaust pipe	η εξάτμιση	i exátmisi
22	seat belt	η ζώνη ασφαλείας	i zóni asfalías
	fan	ο ανεμιστήρας	o anemistíras
23	distributor cables	οι αγωγοί διανομής	i aghoyí dhianomís
24	gear lever	ο λεβιές αλλαγής ταχυτήτων	i levyés alayís tahitíton

25	windscreen	το παρμπρίζ	*to parbríz*
	water pump	η αντλία νερού	*i andlía neróo*
26	wheel	η ρόδα	*i ródha*
27	hubca	το καπάκι της ρόδας	*to kapáki tis ródhas*
	piston	το έμβολο	*to émvolo*

5 .5 The car

See the diagram on page 49.

● **Particular traffic regulations:**
- **maximum speed** for cars:
100km/h on motorways
80km/h outside town centres
50km/h in town centres
- **give way**: all traffic from the right has the right of way.

5 .6 The petrol station

● **Ordinary, super and lead-free petrol** are all available in Greece, as is diesel. DERV is only permitted in taxis

How many kilometres to ___ the next petrol station, please?	Πόσα χιλιόμετρα είναι ως το πλησιέστερο βενζινάδικο; *pósa hilyómetra íne os to plisiéstero venzinádhiko?*
I would like...litres of..., ___ please	Βάλτε μου... λίτρα *váltemoo...lítra*
– super _____	Βάλτε μου... λίτρα σούπερ *váltemoo...lítra sóoper*
– leaded _____	Βάλτε μου... λίτρα απλή βενζίνη *váltemoo...lítra aplí venzíni*
– unleaded_____	Βάλτε μου... λίτρα αμόλυβδη *váltemoo...lítra amólivdhi*
– diesel _____	Βάλτε μου... λίτρα ντήζελ *váltemoo...lítra dízel*
I would like...drachmas' worth of petrol, please.	Θα ήθελα υγραέριο για... δραχμές *tha íthela ighraéryo ya...dhrachmés*
Fill her up, please _____	Γεμίστε το, παρακαλώ *yemísteto, parakaló*
Could you check...?_____	Ελέγξτε το... , παρακαλώ *eléngxte to ... parakaló*
– the oil level _____	Ελέγξτε το λάδι, παρακαλώ *eléngxte to ládhi, parakaló*
– the tyre pressure _____	Ελέγξτε τα λάστιχα, παρακαλώ *eléngxte ta lásticha, parakaló*
Could you change the _____ oil, please?	Μπορείτε να αλλάξετε τα λάδια; *boríte na aláxete ta ládhya?*
Could you clean the _____ windows/the windscreen, please?	Μπορείτε να καθαρίσετε τα τζάμια/το παρ-μπρίζ; *boríte na katharísete ta tzámya/to parbríz?*
Could you give the car_____ a wash, please?	Μπορείτε να πλύνετε το αυτοκίνητο; *boríte na plínete to aftokínito?*

5 .7 Breakdown and repairs

I'm having car trouble _____ Could you give me a hand?	Έπαθα βλάβη. Μπορείτε να με βοηθήσετε; *épatha vlávi. boríte na me voithísete?*
I've run out of petrol _____	Έμεινα από βενζίνη *émina apó venzíni*
I've locked the keys_____ in the car	Έχω αφήσει τα κλειδιά στο αυτοκίνητο *écho afísi ta klidhyá sto aftokínito*

The car/motorbike/ _____ moped won't start	Το αυτοκίνητο/η μοτοσικλέτα/το μηχανάκι δεν παίρνει μπρος
	to aftokínito/i motosikléta/to michanáki dhembérni bros
Could you contact the _____ recovery service for me, please?	Μπορείτε να τηλεφωνήσετε στην ΕΛΠΑ;
	boríte na tilefonísete stin elpá;
Could you call a garage_____ for me, please?	Μπορείτε να τηλεφωνήσετε σ' ένα γκαράζ;
	boríte na tilefonísete séna garáz?
Could you give me _____ a lift...?	Μπορείτε να με πάρετε μαζί σας;
	boríte na me párete mazísas?
– to a garage/into town? ___	Μπορείτε να με πάτε σ' ένα γκαράζ/στην πόλη;
	boríte na me páte séna garáz/stim bóli?
– to a phone booth? _____	Μπορείτε να με πάτε σ' ένα τηλεφωνικό θάλαμο;
	boríte na me páte séna tilefonikó thálamo?
Can we take my _____ bicycle/moped?	Μπορούμε να πάρουμε και το ποδήλατό μου/το μηχανάκι μου;
	boróome na pároome kye to podhílatómoo/to michanákimoo
Could you tow me to _____ a garage?	Μπορείτε να με τραβήξετε σ' ένα γκαράζ;
	boríte na me travíxete séna garáz?
There's probably _____ something wrong with...(See pages 49 and 53)	Πιθανόν να έχει κάτι το...
	pithanón na éhi káti to...
Can you fix it? _____	Μπορείτε να το φτιάξετε;
	boríte na to ftyáxete?
Could you fix my tyre? ____	Μπορείτε να κολλήσετε το λάστιχό μου;
	boríte na kolísete to lastichómoo?
Could you change this_____ wheel?	Μπορείτε ν' αλλάξετε αυτή τη ρόδα;
	boríte naláxete aftí ti ródha?
Can you fix it so it'll _____ get me to...?	Μπορείτε να το φτιάξετε για να μπορώ να πάω μέχρι... ;
	boríte na to ftyáxete ya na boró na páo méchri...?
Which garage can _____ help me?	Ποιό γκαράζ μπορεί να με βοηθήσει;
	pyo garáz borí na me voithísi?
When will my car/bicycle __ be ready?	Πότε θα είναι έτοιμο το αυτοκίνητό μου/το ποδήλατό μου;
	póte tha íne étimo to avtokínitómoo/to podhilatómoo?
Can I wait for it here?_____	Μπορώ να περιμένω εδώ;
	boró na periméno edhó?
How much will it cost? ____	Πόσο θα κοστίσει;
	póso tha kostísi?
Could you confirm the_____ details of the bill?	Μπορείτε να διευκρινήσετε το λογαριασμό;
	boríte na dhiefkrinísete to loghariazmó?
Can I have a receipt for ____ the insurance?	Μπορείτε να μου δώσετε μια απόδειξη για την ασφάλεια;
	boríte na moo dhósete mya apódhixi ya tin asfálya?

The parts of a bicycle

(the diagram shows the numbered parts)

1	rear lamp	το πίσω φως	*to píso fos*
2	rear wheel	η πισινή ρόδα	*i pisiní ródha*
3	(luggage) carrier	η σχάρα	*i schára*
4	bicycle fork	η κεφαλή διχαλωτού άξονος	*i kefalí dhichalotóo áxonos*
5	bell	το κουδούνι	*to koodhóoni*
6	crank	η μανιβέλα	*i manivéla*
7	gear change	η αλλαγή ταχυτήτων	*i alayí tahitíton*
	wire	το συρματάκι	*to sirmatáki*
	dynamo	το δυναμό	*to dhinamó*
	bicycle trailer	το ποδήλατο με ρυμουλκούμενο καροτσάκι	*to podhílato me rimoolkóomeno karotsáki*
	frame	ο σκελετός	*o skeletós*
8	dress guard	ο προφυλακτήρας φορεμάτων	*o profilaktíras foremáton*
9	chain guard	η αλυσίδα	*i alisídha*
	chain lock	η αλυσίδα (για το κλείδωμα του ποδηλάτου)	*i alisídha (ya to klídhoma too podhilátoo)*
	milometer	το κοντέρ	*o kontér*
	child's seat	η παιδική σέλα	*i pedhikí séla*
10	headlamp	το φανάρι	*to fanári*
	bulb	η λάμπα	*i lámpa*
11	pedal	το πηδάλι	*to pidháli*
12	pump	η τρόμπα	*i trómba*
13	reflector	ο πίσω αντανακλαστήρας	*o píso andanaklistíras*
14	break pad	το τακάκι	*to takáki*
15	brake cable	το καλώδιο του φρένου	*to kalódhyo too frénoo*
16	ring lock	η κυκλική κλειδαριά	*i kiklikí klidharyá*
17	carrier straps	τα λουριά της σχάρας	*ta looryá tis scháras*
	tachometer	το ταχύμετρο	*to tahímetro*
18	spoke	η ακτίνα της ρόδας	*i aktína tis ródhas*
19	mudguard	το φτερό	*o fteró*
20	handlebar	το τιμόνι	*to timóni*
21	chain wheel	η ρόδα της αλυσίδας	*i ródha tis alisídhas*
22	crank axle	ο άξονας του πηδαλιού	*too pidhalyóo áxonas*
	rim	η ζάντα	*i zánda*
23	valve	η αεροβαλβίδα	*i aerovalvídha*
24	valve tube	το σωληνάκι της αεροβαλβίδας	*to solináki tis aerovalvídhas*
25	gear cable	το καλώδιο επιτάχυνσης	*to kalódhyo epitáchinsis*
26	front fork	η μπροστινή φουρκέτα	*i brostiní foorkéta*
27	front wheel	η μπροστινή ρόδα	*i brostiní ródha*
28	seat	η σέλα	*i séla*

5 .8 The bicycle/moped

See the diagram on page 53.

● **Cycle paths** are non-existent in Greece, and little consideration for cyclists is shown on the roads. In tourist places bikes and mopeds can be hired at tourist centres. The maximum speed for mopeds is 40km/h, both inside and outside town centres. Passengers may only be carried on small motorcycles clearly designed with a passenger seat. A crash helmet is advisable.

Δεν έχω ανταλλακτικά για το_____ αυτοκίνητό σας/το ποδήλατό σας	I don't have parts for your car/bicycle
Πρέπει να πάρω τα ανταλλακτικά από ____ κάπου αλλού	I have to get the parts from somewhere else
Πρέπει να παραγγείλω τα_____ ανταλλακτικά	I have to order the parts
Αυτό θέλει μισή μέρα _____	That'll take half a day
Αυτό θέλει μια μέρα _____	That'll take a day
Αυτό θέλει μερικές μέρες_____	That'll take a few days
Αυτό θέλει μια εβδομάδα _____	That'll take a week
Το αυτοκίνητό σας είναι εντελώς _____ διαλυμένο	Your car is a write-off
Δεν μπορούμε να κάνουμε τίποτα πια ____	It can't be repaired
Το αυτοκίνητο/η μοτοσικλέτα/το _____ μηχανάκι/το ποδήλατο είναι έτοιμο στις...	The car/motor bike/moped/bicycle will be ready at... o'clock

5 .9 Renting a vehicle

I'd like to rent a..._____	Θα ήθελα να νοικιάσω ένα... *tha íthela na nikyáso éna...*
Do I need a (special)_____ licence for that?	Χρειάζομαι μια (ορισμένη) άδεια οδηγήσεως γι' αυτό; *chriázome mya (orizméni) ádhya odhiyíseos yavtó?*
I'd like to rent the...for... ___	Θέλω να νοικιάσω το... για... *thélo na nikyáso to...ya...*
– one day _____	Θέλω να νοικιάσω το... για μία μέρα *thélo na nikyáso to...ya mía méra*
– two days _____	Θέλω να νοικιάσω το... για δύο μέρες *thélo na nikyáso to...ya dhío méres*
How much is that per_____ day/week?	Πόσο κάνει την ημέρα/την εβδομάδα; *póso káni tin iméra/tin evdhomádha?*
How much is the _____ deposit?	Πόσο είναι η εγγύηση; *póso íne i engíisi?*
Could I have a receipt _____ for the deposit?	Μπορείτε να μου δώσετε μια απόδειξη ότι πλήρωσα την εγγύηση; *boríte ne moo dhósete mya apódhixi óti plírosa tin engíisi?*
How much is the _____ surcharge per kilometre?	Πόσο είναι το συμπληρωματικό ποσό για κάθε χιλιόμετρο; *póso íne to simbliromatikó posó ya káthe hilyómetro?*

Does that include petrol? ___	Είναι αυτό μαζί με τη βενζίνη; *íne aftó mazí me ti venzíni?*
Does that include _____ insurance?	Είναι αυτό μαζί με την ασφάλεια; *íne aftó mazí me tin asfálya?*
What time can I pick_____ the...up tomorrow?	Τί ώρα μπορώ να περάσω αύριο να πάρω το...; *ti óra boró na peráso ávrio na páro to...?*
When does the...have _____ to be back?	Πότε πρέπει να επιστρέψω το... ; *póte prépi na epistrépso to...?*
Where's the petrol tank? ___	Πού βρίσκεται το ρεζερβουάρ; *poo vrískete to rezervvár?*
What sort of fuel does _____ it take?	Τί είδος καύσιμα χρειάζεται; *ti ídhos káfsima chriázete?*

5 .10 Hitchhiking

Where are you heading? ___	Πού πηγαίνετε; *poo piyénete?*
Can I come along? _____	Μπορείτε να με πάρετε μαζί σας; *boríte na me párete mazísas?*
Can my boyfriend/ _____ girlfriend come too?	Μπορείτε να πάρετε και το φίλο μου/τη φίλη μου; *boríte na párete kye to fílomoo/ti fílimoo?*
I'm trying to get to..._____	Εγώ πηγαίνω σε... *eghó piyéno se...*
Is that on the way to...? ____	Βρίσκεται αυτό στο δρόμο για... *vrískete aftó sto dhrómo ya...*
Could you drop me off...? __	Μπορείτε να με αφήσετε σε... ; *boríte na me afísete se...?*
– here? _____	Μπορείτε να με αφήσετε εδώ; *boríte na me afísete edhó?*
– at the exit for...? _____	Μπορείτε να με αφήσετε στην έξοδο για... ; *boríte na me afísete stin éxodho ya...?*
– in the centre?_____	Μπορείτε να με αφήσετε στο κέντρο; *boríte na me afísete sto kéndro?*
– at the next roundabout?__	Μπορείτε να με αφήσετε στην επόμενη ροτόντα; *boríte na me afísete stin epómeni*
Could you stop here, _____ please?	Μπορείτε να σταματήσετε εδώ, παρακαλώ; *boríte na stamatísete edhó, parakaló?*
I'd like to get out here _____	Θέλω να κατεβώ εδώ *thélo na katevó edhó*
Thanks for the lift _____	Ευχαριστώ για την εξυπηρέτηση *efcharistó ya tin exipirétisi*

6

Public transport

Public transport

6 .1 **I**n general

Announcements

Το τρένο για..., που φεύγει στις...έχει ____ καθυστέρηση...λεπτών	The...train to...has been delayed by...minutes
Στη γραμμή...φτάνει τώρα το ____ τρένο για.../από...	The train now arriving at platform...is the...train to.../from...
Στη γραμμή...βρίσκεται ακόμα το ____ τρένο για...	The...train for...is still at platform...
Το τρένο για...φεύγει σήμερα από ____ την πλατφόρμα...	Today the...train to...is due to leave from platform...
Φτάνουμε τώρα στο σταθμό... ____	We're now approaching...

Where does this train ____ go to?	Πού πηγαίνει αυτό το τρένο; *poo piyéni aftó to tréno?*
Does this boat go to...? ____	Αυτό το πλοίο πηγαίνει σε...; *aftó to plío piyéni se ...?*
Can I take this bus to...? ____	Μπορώ να πάω σε...με το λεωφορείο; *boró na páo se ... me to leoforío?*
Does this train stop at...? __	Αυτό το τρένο σταματάει σε...; *aftó to tréno stamatái se ...?*
Is this seat taken/free/ ____ reserved?	Αυτή η θέση είναι πιασμένη/ελεύθερη/κλεισμένη; *aftí i thési íne pyazméni/eléftheri/klizméni?*
I've booked... ____	Έχω κλείσει ... *écho klísi ...*
Could you tell me ____ where I have to get off for...?	Μου λέτε πού πρέπει να κατεβώ για...; *moo léte poo prépi na katevó ya...?*
Could you let me ____ know when we get to...?	Μπορείτε να με προειδοποιήσετε όταν θα φτάνουμε κοντά σε...; *boríte na me proidopiísete ótan tha ftánoome kondá se...?*
Could you stop at the ____ next stop, please?	Μπορείτε να σταματήσετε στην επόμενη στάση, παρακαλώ; *boríte na stamtísete stin epómeni stási, parakaló?*
Where are we now? ____	Πού είμαστε εδώ; *poo ímaste edhó?*
Do I have to get off here? __	Πρέπει να κατεβώ εδώ; *prépi na katevó edhó?*
Have we already ____ passed...?	Περάσαμε κιόλας...; *perásame kyólas...?*
How long have I ____ been asleep?	Πόση ώρα κοιμήθηκα; *pósi óra kimíthika?*
How long does ____ the...stop here?	Πόση ώρα κάνει στάση εδώ το... ; *pósi óra káni stási edhó to...?*

6.2 Questions to passengers

Ticket types

Πρώτη ή δεύτερη θέση;_____	First or second class?
Απλό εισιτήριο ή με επιστροφή; _____	Single or return?
Καπνίζοντες ή μη καπνίζοντες;_____	Smoking or non-smoking?
Στο παράθυρο ή στο διάδρομο; _____	Window or aisle?
Μπροστά ή πίσω;_____	Front or back?
Απλή θέση ή κουκέτα;_____	Seat or couchette?
Πάνω, στη μέση ή κάτω; _____	Top, middle or bottom?
Τουριστική θέση ή μπιζνεσκλάς _____	Tourist class or business class?
Καμπίνα ή απλή θέση; _____	Cabin or seat?
Για ένα ή δύο άτομα;_____	Single or double?
Με πόσα άτομα ταξιδεύετε; _____	How many are travelling?

6.3 Tickets

Can I come back on _____ the same ticket?	Είναι με επιστροφή αυτό το εισιτίριο; *íne me epistrofí aftó to isitírio?*
Can I change on_____ this ticket?	Μπορώ να συνεχίσω μ' αυτό το εισιτίριο; *boró na sinechíso maftó to isitírio?*
How long is this ticket _____ valid for?	Για πόσο καιρό ισχύει αυτό το εισιτίριο; *ya póso kyeró ischíi aftó to isitírio?*
Where can I...? _____	Πού μπορώ να... ; *poo boró na...?*
– buy a ticket? _____	Πού μπορώ να αγοράσω εισιτήριο; *poo boró na aghoráso isitírio?*
– make a reservation? _____	Πού μπορώ να κλείσω θέση; *poo boró na klíso thési?*
– book a flight? _____	Πού μπορώ να κλείσω θέση στο αεροπλάνο; *poo boró na klíso thési sto aeropláno?*
Could I have a...to...,_____ please?	Θέλω ένα...για... *thélo éna...ya...*
– a single _____	Θέλω ένα απλό εισιτήριο για... *thélo éna apló isitírio ya...*
– a return _____	Θέλω ένα μετ επιστροφής για... *thélo éna metepistrofís ya...*
first class _____	πρώτη θέση *próti thési*
second class _____	δεύτερη θέση *dhéfteri thési*
tourist class_____	τουριστική θέση *tooristikí thési*
business class _____	μπιζνεσκλάς *biznesklás*
I'd like to book a _____ seat/couchette/cabin	Θέλω να κλείσω θέση/κρεβάτι/καμπίνα *thélo na klíso thési/kreváti/kabína*
I'd like to book a berth in __ the sleeping car	Θέλω να κλείσω θέση στο βαγκον-λί *thélo na klíso thési sto vagonlí*
top/middle/bottom _____	πάνω/στη μέση/κάτω *páno/sti mési/káto*

Destination

Greek	English
Πού πηγαίνετε;	Where are you travelling to?
Πότε φεύγετε;	When are you leaving?
Το...σας φεύγει στις...	Your...leaves at...
Πρέπει ν' αλλάξετε τρένο	You have to change trains
Πρέπει να κατεβείτε σε...	You have to get off at...
Πρέπει να πάτε μέσω...	You have to travel via...
Η αναχώρηση είναι τη...	The outward journey is on...
Η επιστροφή είναι τη...	The return journey is on...
Πρέπει να επιβιβαστείτε στις... το αργότερο	You have to be on board by...

Inside the vehicle

Το εισιτήριό σας, παρακαλώ	Your ticket, please
Τη βεβαίωση της κράτησης, παρακαλώ	Your reservation, please
Το διαβατήριό σας, παρακαλώ	Your passport, please
Κάθεστε σε λάθος θέση	You're in the wrong seat
Βρίσκεσθε σε λάθος...	You're on/in the wrong...
Αυτή η θέση είναι κλεισμένη	This seat is reserved
Πρέπει να πληρώσετε συμπληρωματικό ποσό	You'll have to pay a supplement
Το... έχει καθυστέρηση... λεπτών	The...has been delayed by...minutes

smoking/no smoking	καπνίζοντες/μη καπνίζοντες *kapnízondes/mi kapnízondes*
by the window	στο παράθυρο *sto paráthiro*
single/double	για ένα άτομο/ για δύο άτομα *ya éna átomo/ya dío átoma*
at the front/back	μπροστά/πίσω *brostá/píso*
There are...of us.	Είμαστε...άτομα *ímaste...átoma*
with a car	Μ' ένα αυτοκίνητο *ména avtokínito*
with a caravan	Μ' ένα τροχόσπιτο *ména trochóspito*
with ... bicycles	Με .. ποδήλατα *me...podhílata*
Do you also have...?	Μήπως έχετε και...; *mípos éhete ke....?*
– season tickets?	Μήπως έχετε και κάρτα πολλαπλών διαδρομών; *mípos éhete ke kárta polaplón dhiadhromón?*
– weekly tickets?	Μήπως έχετε και κάρτα για μια εβδομάδα; *mípos éhete ke kárta ya mya evdhomádha?*
– monthly tickets?	Μήπως έχετε και κάρτα για ένα μήνα; *mípos éhete ke kárta ya éna mína?*

6

Public transport

6 .4 Information

Where's...?	Πού είναι...;
	poo íne...?
Where's the information desk?	Πού είναι το γραφείο πληροφοριών;
	poo íne to ghrafío pliroforyón?
Where can I find a timetable?	Πού είναι ο πίνακας αφίξεων/αναχωρήσεων;
	poo íne o pínakas afíxeon/anachoríseon?
Where's the...desk?	Πού είναι η θυρίδα για...;
	poo íne i thirídha ya...?
Do you have a city map with the bus/the underground routes on it?	Μήπως έχετε ένα χάρτη της πόλης με το δίκτυο λεωφορείων/του μετρό;
	mípos éhete éna chárti tis pólis me to dhíktio leoforíon/too metró?
Do you have a timetable?	Μήπως έχετε το ωράριο των δρομολογίων;
	mípos éhete to orário ton dhromoloyíon?
I'd like to confirm/ cancel/change my booking for/trip to...	Θέλω να επιβεβαιώσω/ακυρώσω/αλλάξω την κράτησή μου/το ταξίδι μου σε...
	thélo na epivevéoso/akiróso/aláxo tingrátisímoo/to taxídhi moo se...
Will I get my money back?	Θα πάρω πίσω τα λεφτά μου;
	tha páro píso ta leftá moo?
I want to go to... What's the quickest way to get there?	Πρέπει να πάω σε ... Πώς πάω εκεί το γρηγορότερο;
	prépi na páo se ... Pos páo ekí to ghrighorótero?
How much is a single/return to...?	Πόσο κάνει ένα απλό εισιτήριο/ένα μετ' επιστροφής;
	póso káni éna apló isitírio/éna metepistrofís?
Do I have to pay a supplement?	Πρέπει να πληρώσω συμπληρωματικό εισιτήριο;
	prépi na pliróso simbliromatikó isitírio?
Can I interrupt my journey with this ticket?	Μπορώ να διακόψω το ταξίδι μου μ' αυτό το εισιτήριο;
	boró na dhiakópso to taxídhimoo maftó to isitírio?
How much luggage am I allowed?	Πόσες αποσκευές μπορώ να πάρω μαζί μου;
	póses aposkevés boró na páro mazímoo?
Does this...travel direct?	Αυτό το...πηγαίνει κατ' ευθείαν;
	aftó to...piyéni katefthían?
Do I have to change trains/buses/boats? Where?	Πρέπει ν' αλλάξω τρένο/λεωφορείο/πλοίο; Πού;
	prépi naláxo tréno/leoforío/plío? Poo?
Does the plane touch down anywhere en route?	Το αεροπλάνο κάνει ενδιάμεσες προσγειώσεις;
	to aeropláno káni endhiámeses prosyiósis?
Does the boat call in at any ports on the way?	Το πλοίο πιάνει σκάλα και σ' άλλα λιμάνια;
	to plío pyáni skála ke sála limánya?
Does the train/ bus stop at...?	Το τρένο/το λεωφορείο κάνει στάση σε...;
	to tréno/to leoforío káni stási se...?
Where should I get off?	Πού πρέπει να κατεβώ;
	poo prépi na katevó?
Is there a connection to...?	Υπάρχει ανταπόκριση για ...
	ipárchi andapókrisi ya...
How long do I have to wait?	Πόση ώρα πρέπει να περιμένω;
	pósi óra prépi na periméno?
When does...leave?	Πότε φεύγει...;
	póte févyi...?

What time does the _____ first/last/next...leave?	Τί ώρα φεύγει το πρώτο/τελευταίο/επόμενο...; *ti óra févyi to próto/teleftéo/epómeno...?*
How long does...take? _____	Πόση ώρα κάνει το...; *pósi óra káni to...?*
What time does...arrive _____ in...?	Τί ώρα φτάνει το...σε...; *ti óra ftáni to...se...?*
Where does the...to... _____ leave from?	Από πού φεύγει το...για...; *apó poo févyi to...ya...?*
Is this...to...? _____	Αυτό είναι το...για...; *aftó íne to...ya...?Δ·b̦!*

6 .5 Aeroplanes

● **In addition to** scheduled flights from the UK to Athens and Thessaloniki there are a large number of charters to both cities and to Corfu, Kos, Crete and Rhodes. Athens has two airports, one for Olympic Airways and one for other airlines; the two airports are quite close to one another. They have two areas, *αφίξεις* (arrivals) and *αναχωρήσεις* (departures). At the check-in desk you will receive a *δελτίο επιβιβασεως* (boarding card) and will be told which *έξοδος* (gate) you will be leaving from

In a Greek airport you will find the following signs:

αναχωρήσεις **departures**	εσωτερικές ανταποκρίσεις **internal/domestic**	πτήσεις εξωτερικού **international flights**
αφίξεις **arrivals**	**connecting flights**	πτήσεις εσωτερικού **domestic flights**

6 .6 Trains

● **The rail network** in Greece is not very extensive, but rail travel is generally much cheaper than in the UK. The Greek State Railways company is responsible for the line from Thessaloniki to Athens. Much of the route is single track, and there are innumerable small stations. Another company runs the loop of track from Athens around the Peloponnese. You can travel first or second class, and students, children and groups of more than ten persons can obtain reductions. It is advisable to book a seat at the time you purchase your ticket.

6 .7 Taxis

● **There are plenty** of taxis in Greece and they are usually much cheaper than in the UK. In Athens and Thessaloniki taxis act rather like buses; they pick up and drop off passengers en route. Virtually all taxis have a meter, but it is often possible to agree a price for a longer journey in advance. A supplement is usual for luggage, a journey at night, on a Sunday or bank holiday, or to an airport.

Taxi! _____	ταξί *taxí!*
Could you get me a taxi, ___ please?	Μπορείτε να καλέσετε ένα ταξί για μένα; *boríte na kalésete éna taxí ya ména?*
Where can I find a taxi_____ around here?	Πού μπορώ να βρω ένα ταξί εδώ κοντά; *poo boró na vro éna taxí edhó kondá?*

ελεύθερο	κατειλημμένο	σταθμός ταξί
free	taken	taxi rank

Could you take me to..., ___   Με πηγαίνετε σε..., παρακαλώ;
please?   *me piyénete se..., parakaló?*

– this address _____   Με πηγαίνετε σ' αυτή τη διεύθυνση,
   παρακαλώ;
   me piyénete saftí ti diéfthinsi, parakaló?

– the...hotel _____   Με πηγαίνετε στο ξενοδοχείο..., παρακαλώ;
   me piyénete sto xenodhohío..., parakaló?

– the town/city centre_____   Με πηγαίνετε στο κέντρο, παρακαλώ;
   me piyénete sto kéndro, parakaló?

– the station _____   Με πηγαίνετε στο σταθμό, παρακαλώ;
   me piyénete sto stathmó, parakaló?

– the airport _____   Με πηγαίνετε στο αεροδρόμιο, παρακαλώ;
   me piyénete sto aerodhrómio, parakaló?

How much is the _____   Πόσο κάνει η διαδρομή μέχρι...;
trip to...?   *póso káni i dhiadromí méchri...?*

How far is it to...? _____   Πόσο μακριά είναι μέχρι... ;
   póso makriá íne méchri...?

Could you turn on the ____   Μπορείτε να βάλετε το μετρητή, παρακαλώ;
meter, please?   *boríte na válete to metrití, parakaló?*

I'm in a hurry _____   Βιάζομαι
   vyázome

Could you speed up/slow __   Μπορείτε να πηγαίνετε πιο γρήγορα/πιο
down a little?   αργά, παρακαλώ;
   boríte na piyénete pyo ghríghora/pyo arghá,
   parakaló?

Could you take a _____   Μπορείτε να πάρετε ένα άλλο δρόμο;
different route?   *boríte na párete éna álo dhrómo?*

I'd like to get out here,____   Αφήστε με να κατεβώ εδώ, παρακαλώ
please   *afíste me na katevó edhó, parakaló*

You have to go...here ____   Εδώ πρέπει να πάτε...
   edhó prépi na páte...

You have to go straight ____   Εδώ πρέπει να πάτε ίσια
on here   *edhó prépi na páte ísya*

You have to turn left_____   Εδώ πρέπει να πάτε αριστερά
here   *edhó prépi na páte aristerá*

You have to turn right ____   Εδώ πρέπει να πάτε δεξιά
here   *edhó prépi na páte dhexyá*

This is it _____   Εδώ είναι
   edhó íne

Could you wait a minute___   Μπορείτε να με περιμένετε ένα λεπτό;
for me, please?   *boríte na me periménete éna leptó?*

6

Public transport

7 Overnight accommodation

Overnight accommodation

7.1 General

● **Hotel accommodation:** hotels (ξενοδοχεία) are in different categories: luxury class, A class, B class, C class, D class, and E class. The classification is somewhat arbitrary, and it is always worth trying a cheap hotel. An expensive hotel will not necessarily be more pleasant or comfortable than a cheaper one.

Most hotels serve breakfast.

Rooms in private houses or pensions are available and offer a cheap and interesting form of accommodation. This is the best way to get to know Greeks. The tourist police can supply you with a list of rooms available in a particular place.

Motels are rare in Greece; they are only to be found close to the motorways.

Youth Hostels exist in the cities; they are divided into male and female sections.

Camping sites are regulated by the Greek National Tourist office (EOT). They are divided into three price levels. There are many sites along the coasts, but they are rarer inland. It is not legal to camp outside such sites.

Πόσο καιρό θέλετε να μείνετε; _____	How long will you be staying?
Μπορείτε να συμπληρώσετε αυτό _____ το έντυπο, παρακαλώ	Fill out this form, please
Το διαβατήριό σας, παρακαλώ _____	Could I see your passport?
Πρέπει να πληρώσετε εγγύηση _____	I'll need a deposit
Πρέπει να προπληρώσετε _____	You'll have to pay in advance

My name's...I've made ____ a reservation over the phone/by mail	Το όνομά μου είναι...'Εκλεισα (τηλεφωνικώς/γραπτά) μια θέση *to ónomámou íne ... éklisa (tilefonikós/ghraptá) mya thési*
How much is it per _____ night/week/ month?	Πόσο κάνει τη νύχτα/την εβδομάδα/το μήνα; *póso káni ti níchta/tin evdhomádha/to mína?*
We'll be staying at _____ least...nights/weeks	Θα μείνουμε τουλάχιστον...νύχτες/εβδομάδες *tha mínoome tooláchiston...níchtes/evdhomádhes*
We don't know yet _____	Δεν ξέρουμε ακόμα ακριβώς *dhen xéroome akóma akrivós*
Do you allow pets _____ (cats/dogs)?	Επιτρέπονται τα κατοικίδια ζώα; *epitréponde ta katikídhia zóa?*
What time does the _____ gate/door open/close?	Τι ώρα κλείνει/ανοίγει η εξώπορτα/η πόρτα; *ti óra klíni/aníyi i exóporta/i pórta?*
Could you get me a taxi, ____ please?	Μου φωνάζετε ένα ταξί, παρακαλώ; *moo fonázete éna taxí, parakaló?*
Where's the manager? ____	Πού είναι ο διαχειριστής; *poo íne o dhiahiristís?*

Overnight accommodation

7.2 Camping

See the diagram on page 67.

Διαλέξετε μόνος σας το μέρος _____	You can pick your own site
Εμείς θα σας δείξουμε ένα μέρος _____	You'll be allocated a site
Αυτός είναι ο αριθμός του μέρους σας ___	This is your site number
Να κολλήσετε αυτό στο _____ αυτοκίνητό σας	Stick this on your car, please
Να μην χάσετε αυτή την κάρτα _____	Please don't lose this card

Are we allowed to _____ camp here?	Μπορούμε να κατασκηνώσουμε εδώ; *boróome na kataskinósoome edhó?*
There are...of us and _____ ...tents	Είμαστε...άτομα και...σκηνές *ímaste...átoma ke...skinés*
Can we pick our_____ own site?	Μπορούμε να διαλέξουμε μόνοι μας ένα μέρος; *boróome na dhialéxoome mónimas éna méros?*
Do you have a quiet _____ spot for us?	'Εχετε ένα ήσυχο μέρος για μας; *éhete éna ísicho méros ya mas?*
Do you have any other ____ sites available?	Δεν έχετε ένα άλλο μέρος ελεύθερο; *dhen éhete éna álo méros eléfthero?*
It's too windy/sunny/ _____ shady here	'Εχει πολύ αέρα/ήλιο/ίσκιο εδώ *éhi polí aéra/ílyo/ískyo edhó*
It's too crowded here _____	'Εχει πολλή κίνηση εδώ *éhi polí kínisi edhó*
The ground's too _____ hard/uneven	Το έδαφος είναι πολύ σκληρό/άνισο *to édhafos íne polí skliró/ániso*
Do you have a level _____ spot for the camper/caravan/folding caravan?	'Εχετε ένα ίσιο μέρος για το κάμπερ μας/το τροχόσπιτο μας. το λυόμενο τροχόσπιτό μας; *éhete éna ísyo méros ya to kámpermas/to trochóspitómas /to liómeno trochóspitómas*
Could we have adjoining __ pitches?	Μπορούμε να κατασκηνώσουμε δίπλα-δίπλα; *boróome na kataskinósoome dhípla-dhípla?*
Can we park the car _____ next to the tent?	Μπορώ να παρκάρω το αυτοκίνητο δίπλα στη σκηνή; *boró na parkáro to aftokínito dhípla sti skiní?*
How much is it per _____ person/tent/caravan/car?	Πόσο κάνει το άτομο/για μία σκηνή/για ένα τροχόσπιτο/για ένα αυτοκίνητο; *póso káni to átomo/ya mía skiní/ya éna trochóspito/ya éna aftokínito?*
Are there any chalets to ___ rent?	Νοικιάζονται καλύβες; *nikyázonde kalíves?*
Are there any...?_____	Υπάρχουν εδώ...; *ipárchoon edhó...?*
– any hot showers?_____	Υπάρχουν εδώ ντους με ζεστό νερό *ipárchoon edhó doos me zestó neró*
– washing machines?_____	Υπάρχουν εδώ πλυντήρια; *ipárchoon edhó plindíria?*
Is there a...on the site?_____	Υπάρχει σ' αυτό το χώρο...; *ipárchi saftó to chóro...?*
Is there a children's_____ play area on the site?	Υπάρχει σ' αυτό το χώρο μια παιδική χαρά; *ipárchi saftó to chóro mya pedhikí chará?*

7 Overnight accommodation

Camping equipment
(the diagram shows the numbered parts)

luggage space	ο χώρος αποσκευών	o chóros aposkevón l
can opener	το ανοιχτήρι	to anichtíri
butane gas bottle	η μποτίλια υγραερίου	i botílya ighraeríoo
1 pannier	η τσάντα του ποδηλάτου	i tsánda too podilátoo
2 gas cooker	η κουζίνα υγραερίου	i koozína ighraeríoo
3 groundsheet	το πάτωμα της σκηνής	to pátoma tis skinís
mallet	το σφυρί	to sfirí
hammock	η μπράντα	i bránda
4 jerry can	το μπιντόνι	to bidóni
campfire	η πυρά	i pirá
5 folding chair	η πτυσσόμενη καρέκλα	i ptisómeni karékla
6 insulated picnic box	η τσάντα-ψυγείο	i tsánda-psiyío
ice pack	ο ψυκτήρας	o psiktíras
compass	η πυξίδα	i pixídha
wick	το φυτίλι	to fitíli
corkscrew	το τιρμπουσόν	to tirboosón
7 airbed	το αερόστρωμα	to aeróstroma
8 airbed plug	το βούλωμα του αεροστρώματος	to vóoloma too aerostrómatos
pump	το ποδοκίνητο φυσερό	to podhokinitó fiseró
9 awning	το προστέγασμα της σκηνής	to prostéghazma tis skinís
10 karimat	το χαλάκι	to chaláki
11 pan	η κατσαρόλα	i katsaróla
12 pan handle	το χερούλι	to heróoli
primus stove	η γκαζιέρα	i gazyéra
zip	το φερμουάρ	to fermwár
13 backpack	το σακίδιο	to sakídhyo
14 guy rope	το σχοινί της σκηνής	to schiní tis skinís
sleeping bag	ο υπνόσακος	o ipnósekos
15 storm lantern	η λάμπα θύελλας	i lámpa thíelas
camp bed	το ράντζο	to rántso
table	το τραπέζι	to trapézi
16 tent	η σκηνή	i skiní
17 tent peg	το πασαλάκι της σκηνής	to pasaláki tis skinís
18 tent pole	ο ορθοστάτης της σκηνής	o orthostátis tis skinís
vacuum flask	το θερμός	to thermós
19 water bottle	το παγούρι	to paghóori
clothes peg	το μανταλάκι	to mandaláki
clothes line	το σχοινί της μπουγάδας	to schiní tis booghádhas
windbreak	ο ανεμοφράκτης	o anemofráktis
20 torch	ο φακός	o fakós
pocket knife	ο σουγιάς	o sooyás

English	Greek
Are there covered _____ cooking facilities on the site?	Υπάρχει σκεπαστός χώρος για μαγείρευμα; *ipárchi skepastós chóros ya mayírevma?*
Can I rent a safe here? _____	Μπορώ να νοικιάσω ένα χρηματοκιβώτιο; *boró na nikyáso éna chrimatokivótyo?*
Are we allowed to _____ barbecue here?	Επιτρέπεται εδώ το μπάρμπεκιου; *epitrépete edhó to barbekyóo?*
Are there any power _____ points?	Υπάρχουν ηλεκτρικές συνδέσεις; *ipárchoon ilektrikés sindhésis?*
Is there drinking water? _____	Υπάρχει πόσιμο νερό; *ipárchi pósimo neró?*
When's the rubbish _____ collected?	Πότε μαζεύουν τα σκουπίδια; *póte mazévoon ta skoopídhya?*
Do you sell gas bottles (butane gas/propane gas)?	Πουλάτε φιάλες υγραερίου (πετρογκάζ); *pooláte fyáles ighraeríoo (petrogáz)?*

.3 Hotel/B&B/apartment/holiday house

English	Greek
Do you have a _____ single/double room available?	Έχετε ένα ελεύθερο μονό/διπλό δωμάτιο; *éhete éna eléfthero monó/dhipló dhomátyo?*
per person/per room _____	το άτομο/το δωμάτιο *to átomo/to dhomátyo*
Does that include _____ breakfast/lunch/dinner?	Με το πρωινό/το μεσημεριανό/το βραδινό; *me to proinó/to mesimeryanó/to vradhinó?*
Could we have two _____ adjoining rooms?	Μπορούμε να έχουμε δύο δωμάτια δίπλα-δίπλα; *boróome na échoome dhío dhomátya dhípla-dhípla?*
with/without _____ toilet/bath/shower	με/χωρίς τουαλέτα/μπάνιο/ντους *me/chorís twaléta/bányo/doos*
(not) facing the street _____	(όχι) από την μεριά του δρόμου *(óhi) apó ti meryá too dhrómoo*
with/without a view _____ of the sea	με/χωρίς θέα προς τη θάλασσα *me/chorís théa pros ti thálasa*
Is there...in the hotel? _____	Το ξενοδοχείο έχει...; *to xenodhohío éhi...?*
Is there a lift in the hotel? _	Το ξενοδοχείο έχει ασανσέρ; *to xenodhohío éhi asansér?*
Do you have _____ room service?	Το ξενοδοχείο έχει εξυπηρέτηση δωματίου/ρουμ σέρβις; *to xenodhohío éhi exipirétisi dhomatíoo/room sérvis?*
Could I see the room? _____	Μπορώ να δω το δωμάτιο; *boró na dho to dhomátyo?*
I'll take this room _____	Θα πάρω αυτό το δωμάτιο *tha páro aftó to dhomátyo*
We don't like this one _____	Αυτό το δωμάτιο δε μας αρέσει *aftó to dhomátyo dhe mas arési*
Do you have a larger/_____ less expensive room?	Έχετε ένα μεγαλύτερο/πιο φτηνό δωμάτιο; *éhete éna meghalítero/pyo ftinó dhomátyo?*
Could you put in a cot? _____	Μπορείτε να βάλετε κι ένα παιδικό κρεβάτι στο δωμάτιό μας; *boríte na válete kyéna pedhikó kreváti sto dhomátiómas?*
What time's breakfast? _____	Τί ώρα είναι το πρωινό; *ti óra íne to proinó?*

Where's the dining room?	Πού είναι η τραπεζαρία;
	poo íne i trapezaría?
Can I have breakfast in my room?	Μπορώ να έχω το πρωινό στο δωμάτιό μου;
	boró na écho to proinó sto dhomátiómoo?
Where's the emergency exit/fire escape?	Πού είναι η έξοδος κινδύνου ή η σκάλα πυρκαγιάς;
	poo íne i éxodhos kindhínoo/i skála pirkayás?

Η τουαλέτα και το ντους είναι _____ στον ίδιο όροφο/στο δωμάτιό σας	You can find the toilet and shower on the same floor/en suite
Από δω, παρακαλώ _____	This way, please
Το δωμάτιό σας είναι στο...όροφο, _____ ο αριθμός είναι...	Your room is on the...floor, number...

Where can I park my car (safely)?	Υπάρχει ένα (ασφαλές) μέρος όπου μπορώ να παρκάρω το αυτοκίνητό μου;
	ipárchi éna (asfalés) méros όpoo boró na parkáro to aftokínitómoo?
The key to room..., please	Το κλειδί του δωματίου..., παρακαλώ
	to klidhí too dhomatíoo..., parakaló
Could you put this in the safe, please?	Μπορώ να αφήσω αυτό στο χρηματοκιβώτιό σας;
	boró nafíso aftó sto chrimatokivótiósas?
Could you wake me at...tomorrow?	Μπορείτε να με ξυπνήσετε αύριο στις...;
	boríte na me xipnísete ávrio stis ...?
Could you find a babysitter for me?	Μπορείτε να μου βρείτε μια μπέιμπυ σίτερ;
	boríte na moo vríte mya béibi-síter?
Could I have an extra blanket?	Μπορώ να έχω κι άλλη μια κουβέρτα;
	boró na écho kyáli mía koovérta?
What days do the cleaners come in?	Ποιές μέρες καθαρίζουν τα δωμάτια;
	pyes méres katharízoon ta dhomátya?
When are the sheets/towels/tea towels changed?	Πότε αλλάζουν τα σεντόνια/τις πετσέτες/τις πετσέτες για τα πιάτα;
	póte alázoon ta sendónya/tis petsétes/tis petsétes ya ta pyáta?

.4 Complaints

We can't sleep for the noise	Δεν μπορούμε να κοιμηθούμε μ' αυτό το θόρυβο
	dhemboróome na kimithóome maftó to thórivo
Could you turn the radio down, please?	Μπορείτε να χαμηλώσετε λίγο το ραδιόφωνο;
	boríte na chamilósete lígho to radhiófono?
We're out of toilet paper	Τελείωσε το χαρτί υγείας
	telíose to chartí iyías
There aren't any.../there's not enough...	Δεν έχει/δεν έχει αρκετά...
	dhen éhi/dhen éhi arketá...
The bed linen's dirty	Τα κλινοσκεπάσματα είναι βρώμικα
	ta klinoskepázmata íne vrómika
The room hasn't been cleaned	Δεν καθάρισαν το δωμάτιο
	dhen kathárisan to dhomátyo

The kitchen is not clean____	Η κουζίνα δεν είναι καθαρή
	i koozína dhen íne katharí
The kitchen utensils are____ dirty	Τα κουζινικά είναι βρώμικα
	ta kooziniká íne vrómika
The heater's not_____ working	Το καλοριφέρ δε λειτουργεί
	to kalorifér dhe litooryí
There's no (hot) _____ water/electricity	Δεν έχει (ζεστό) νερό/ρεύμα
	dhen éhi (zestó) neró/révma
...is broken_____	...χάλασε
	...chálase
Could you have that_____ seen to?	Μπορείτε να το διορθώσετε;
	boríte na to dhiorthósete?
Could I have another _____ room?	Μπορείτε να μου δώσετε ένα άλλο δωμάτιο
	boríte na moo dhósete éna álo dhomátyo
The bed creaks terribly ____	Το κρεβάτι τρίζει φοβερά
	to kreváti trízi foverá
The bed sags terribly _____	Το κρεβάτι βουλιάζει φοβερά
	to kreváti voolyázi foverá
There's a lot of noise _____	Έχει πάρα πολύ θόρυβο
	éhi pára polí thórivo
There are bugs/insects____ in our room	Έχουμε πολλά ζωύφια/έντομα
	échoome polá zoífya/éndoma
This place is full_____ of mosquitos	Είναι γεμάτο κουνούπια εδώ
	íne yemáto koonóopya edhó
– cockroaches_____	Είναι γεμάτο κατσαρίδες εδώ
	íne yemáto katsarídhes edhó

.5 Departure

See also 8.2 Settling the bill

I'm leaving tomorrow. _____ Could I settle my bill, please?	Αύριο φεύγω. Μπορώ να πληρώσω τώρα;
	ávrio févgho. boró na pliróso tóra?
What time should we_____ vacate?	Τι ώρα πρέπει να φύγουμε από...;
	ti óra prépi na fíghoome apó...?
Could I have my deposit/ __ passport back, please?	Μου δίνετε πίσω την εγγύηση/το διαβατήριό μου;
	moo dhínete píso tin engíisi/to dhiavatíriómoo?
We're in a terrible hurry ___	Βιαζόμαστε πολύ
	vyazómaste polí
Could you forward _____ my mail to this address?	Μπορείτε να στείλετε τα γράμματά μου σ' αυτή τη διεύθυνση;
	boríte na stílete ta ghrámatámoo saftí ti dhiéfthinsi?
Could we leave our_____ luggage here until we leave?	Μπορούμε να αφήσουμε τις βαλίτσες μας εδώ μέχρι να φύγουμε;
	boróome nafísoome tis valítses mas edhó méchri na fíghoome?
Thanks for your _____ hospitality	Ευχαριστώ για τη φιλοξενία σας
	efcharistó ya ti filoxeníasas

Overnight accommodation

Money matters

8 Money matters

● **In general,** banks are open to the public between 8am and 2pm; they are closed on Saturdays. Exchange bureaux are open until 10pm. Money and travellers cheques can also be changed in most of the larger hotels. In the islands the post-offices often have currency changing facilities. To exchange currency a proof of identity is usually required. The sign *ΣΥΝΑΛΛΑΓΜΑ* indicates that money can be exchanged.

8.1 Banks

Where can I find a _____ bank/an exchange office around here?	Υπάρχει εδώ κοντά καμιά τράπεζα/κανένα γραφείο συναλλάγματος; *ipárchi edhó kondá kamyá trápeza/kanéna ghrafío sinalághmatos?*
Where can I cash this _____ traveller's cheque/giro cheque?	Πού μπορώ να εξαργυρώσω αυτή την ταξιδιωτική επιταγή/ταχυδρομική επιταγή; *poo boró na exaryiróso aftí tin taxidhiotikí epitayí/ tachidhromikí epitayí?*
Can I cash this...here? _____	Μπορώ εδώ να εξαργυρώσω αυτό το...; *boró edhó na exaryiróso avtó to...?*
Can I withdraw money _____ on my credit card here?	Μπορώ να πάρω λεφτά εδώ με μια πιστωτική κάρτα; *boró na páro leftá edhó me mya pistotikí kárta?*
What's the minimum/ _____ maximum amount?	Ποιό είναι το ελάχιστο ποσό/το ανώτατο ποσό; *pyo íne to eláchisto posó/to anótato posó?*
Can I take out less _____ than that?	Μπορώ να πάρω και μικρότερο ποσό; *boró na páro ke mikrótero posó?*
I've had some money _____ transferred here. Has it arrived yet?	Έκανα ένα τηλεγραφικό έμβασμα. Έφτασε το έμβασμα; *ékana éna tileghrafikó émvazma. éftase to émvazma?*
These are the details _____ of my bank in the UK	Αυτά είναι τα στοιχεία της τράπεζάς μου στο Ηνωμένο Βασίλειο *aftá íne ta stihía tis trápezásmoo sto Inoméno Vasílio*
This is my bank/giro _____ number	Αυτός είναι ο αριθμός λογαριασμού μου *aftós íne o arithmós loghariazmóomoo*
I'd like to change _____ some money	Θα ήθελα ν' αλλάξω χρήματα *tha íthela naláxo chrímata*
– pounds into... _____	λίρες στερλίνες για... *líres sterlínes ya...*
– dollars into... _____	δολλάρια για... *dholária ya...*
What's the exchange _____ rate?	Ποιά είναι η ισοτιμία; *pya íne i isotimía?*
Could you give me _____ some small change with it?	Μπορείτε να μου δώσετε και λίγα ψιλά, παρακαλώ; *boríte na moo dhósete ke lígha psilá, parakaló?*
This is not right _____	Αυτό είναι λάθος *avtó íne láthos*

Υπογράψετε εδώ_____	Sign here, please.
Συμπληρώσετε αυτό το χαρτί_____	Fill this out, please.
Μπορώ να δω το διαβατήριό σας; _____	Could I see your passport, please?
Μπορώ να δω την ταυτότητά σας; _____	Could I see some identification, please?
Μπορώ να δω την ταχυδρομική _____ σας κάρτα;	Could I see your girobank card, please?
Μπορώ να δω την τραπεζική _____ σας κάρτα;	Could I see your bank card, please?

8 .2 Settling the bill

Could you put it on_____ my bill?	Μπορείτε να το γράψετε στο λογαριασμό μου;
	boríte na to ghrápsete sto loghariazmómoo?
Does this amount _____ include service?	(Στο ποσό αυτό) συμπεριλαμβάνεται η εξυπηρέτηση;
	(sto posó aftó) simberilamvánete i exipirétisi?
Can I pay by...?_____	Μπορώ να πληρώσω με...;
	boró na plíroso me...?
Can I pay by credit card?___	Μπορώ να πληρώσω με πιστωτική κάρτα;
	boró na plíroso me pistotikí kárta?
Can I pay by traveller's ____ cheque?	Μπορώ να πληρώσω με ταξιδιωτική επιταγή;
	boró na plíroso me taxidhyotikí epitayí?
Can I pay with foreign _____ currency?	Μπορώ να πληρώσω με ξένο συνάλλαγμα;
	boró na plíroso me xéno sinálaghma?
You've given me too _____ much/you haven't given me enough change	Μου δώσατε πίσω πάρα πολλά/πολύ λίγα
	moo dhósate píso pára polá/polí lígha

Δε δεχόμαστε πιστωτικές _____ κάρτες/ταξιδιωτικές επιταγές/ξένο συνάλλαγμα	We don't accept credit cards/traveller's cheques/foreign currency

Could you check this _____ again, please?	Μπορείτε να το ξαναελέγξετε, παρακαλώ;
	boríte na to xanaelénxete, parakaló?
Could I have a receipt, ____ please?	Μπορώ να έχω μια απόδειξη/το λογαριασμό;
	boró na écho mya apódhixi/to loghariazmó?
I don't have enough _____ money on me	Δεν έχω αρκετά χρήματα επάνω μου
	dhen écho arketá chrímata epánomoo
This is for you _____	ορίστε, αυτό είναι για σας
	oríste, aftó íne ya sas
Keep the change _____	Κρατήστε τα ρέστα
	kratíste ta résta

Post and telephone

Post and telephone

 .1 Post

For giros, see 8 Money matters

● **In large towns** post offices are open from Monday to Friday between 7.30am and 8pm; in many such towns they are also open on Saturdays. In smaller towns the opening times are variable. Greek post-offices can be recognised by the sign ΕΛΤΑ. Giro cards can be used there.

Stamps (*γραμματόσημα*) are also available in kiosks (*περίπτερα*) and in tourist areas they are often also sold in small souvenir and postcard shops.

γραμματόσημα	ταχυδρομικές επιταγές	τηλεγραφήματα
stamps	**money orders**	**telegrams**
δέματα		
parcels		

Where's...? _____	Πού είναι...;
	poo íne...?
Where's the post office? ___	Υπάρχει εδώ κοντά κανένα ταχυδρομείο;
	ipárchi edhó kondá kanéna tahidhromío?
Where's the main post____ office?	Πού είναι το κεντρικό ταχυδρομείο;
	poo íne to kendrikó tahidhromío?
Where's the postbox? _____	Υπάρχει εδώ κοντά ένα γραμματοκιβώτιο;
	ipárchi edhó kondá éna ghramatokivótyo?
Which counter should _____ I go to...?	Σε ποιά θυρίδα πρέπει να πάω για...;
	se pya thirídha prépi na páo ya...?
– to send a fax _____	Σε ποιά θυρίδα πρέπει να πάω για να στείλω ένα φαξ;
	se pya thirídha prépi na páo ya na stílo éna fax?
– to change money_____	Σε ποιά θυρίδα πρέπει να πάω για να αλλάξω χρήματα;
	se pya thirídha prépi na páo ya naláxo chrímata?
– to change giro cheques __	Σε ποιά θυρίδα πρέπει να πάω για να εξαργυρώσω τα ταχυδρομικά τσεκ;
	se pya thirídha prépi na páo ya na exaryiróso ta tahidhromiká tsek?
– for a Telegraph Money ___ Order?	Σε ποιά θυρίδα πρέπει να πάω για τηλεγραφικό έμβασμα;
	se pya thirídha prépi na páo ya tileghrafikó émvazma?
Poste restante_____	Ποστ-ρεστάντ
	post-restánt
Is there any mail for me? __ My name's...	Έχετε γράμματα για μένα; Το όνομά μου είναι...
	éhete ghrámata ya ména? to ónomámoo íne...

Stamps

What's the postage _____ for a...to...?	Τί γραμματόσημα χρειάζομαι για...; *ti ghramatósima chriázome ya...?*
Are there enough _____ stamps on it?	Φτάνουν αυτά τα γραμματόσημα; *ftánoon aftá ta ghramatósima*
I'd like... ...drachma _____ stamps	Θα ήθελα...γραμματόσημα των... *tha íthela...ghramatósima ton...*
I'd like to send this... _____	Θέλω να το στείλω αυτό ... *thélo na to stílo aftó...*
– express _____	Θέλω να το στείλω αυτό επείγον *thélo na to stílo aftó epíghon*
– by air mail _____	Θέλω να το στείλω αυτό αεροπορικώς *thélo na to stílo aftó aeroporikós*
– by registered mail _____	Θέλω να το στείλω αυτό συστημένο *thélo na to stílo aftó sistiméno*

Telegram / fax

I'd like to send a _____ telegram to...	Θα ήθελα να στείλω ένα τηλεγράφημα σε... *tha íthela na stílo éna tileghráfima se...*
How much is that _____ per word?	Πόσο κάνει η λέξη; *póso káni i léxi?*
This is the text I want _____ to send	Αυτό είναι το κείμενο που θέλω να στείλω *aftó íne to kímeno poo thélo na stílo*
Shall I fill out the form _____ myself?	Να συμπληρώσω μόνος/μόνη μου το έντυπο; *na simpliróso mónos/móni moo to éndipo?*
Can I make photocopies/___ send a fax here?	Μπορώ να κάνω φωτοτυπίες/να στείλω ένα φαξ; *boró edhó na káno fototipíes/na stílo éna fax?*
How much is it _____ per page?	Πόσο κάνει η σελίδα; *póso káni i selídha?*

9 .2 Telephone

See also 1.8 Telephone alphabet

● **In Greece** you cannot make phone calls from an ordinary post office. The special telephone offices are marked OTE. Here you make the call and then pay. In tourist resorts there are usually a number of public phone-boxes (for which a phone-card is advisable) from which you can make international calls, and local calls can be made from kiosks.

When phoning someone in Greece, you will not be greeted with the subscriber's name or number, but simply with *εμπρός* or *ορίστε*.

Is there a phone box _____ around here?	Υπάρχει εδώ κοντά κανένας τηλεφωνικός θάλαμος; *ipárchi edhó kondá kanénas tilefonikós thálamos?*
Could I use your _____ phone, please?	Μπορώ να χρησιμοποιήσω το τηλέφωνό σας; *boró na chrisimopiíso to tiléfonósas?*
Do you have a _____ (city/region)...phone directory?	Εχετε ένα τηλεφωνικό κατάλογο της πόλης.../της περιοχής...; *éhete éna tilefonikó katálogho tis pólis/tis periohís...?*
Could you give me...? _____	Μπορείτε να μου δώσετε...; *boríte na moo dhósete...?*

– the number for _____ Μπορείτε να μου δώσετε τον αριθμό για τις
international directory πληροφορίες εξωτερικού;
enquiries *boríte na moo dhósete ton airithmó ya tis
plirofories exoterikóo?*

– the number of room... ___ Μπορείτε να μου δώσετε τον αριθμό του
δωματίου;
*boríte na moo dhósete ton arithmó too
dhomatíoo...?*

– the international _____ Μπορείτε να μου δώσετε το διεθνή κωδικό
access code της/του/των...;
*boríte na moo dhósete to dhiethní kódhiko
tis/too/ton...?*

– the country code for...____ Μπορείτε να μου δώσετε τον κωδικό της...;
boríte na moo dhósete tongódhiko tis...?

– the trunk code for... _____ Μπορείτε να μου δώσετε τον κωδικό της
πόλης...;
boríte na moo dhósete tongódhiko tis pólis...?

– the number of... _____ Μπορείτε να μου δώσετε τον αριθμό
τηλεφώνου του/της...;
*boríte na moo dhósete ton arithmó tilefónoo
too/tis...?*

Could you check if this ____ Μπορείτε να ελέγξετε αν είναι σωστός
number's correct? αυτός ο αριθμός;
boríte na elénxete an íne sostós o arithmós?

Can I dial international____ Μπορώ να τηλεφωνήσω αυτόματα στο
direct? εξωτερικό;
boró na tilefoníso aftómata sto exoterikó?

Do I have to go through __ Πρέπει να τηλεφωνήσω μέσω της
the switchboard? τηλεφωνήτριας;
prépi na tilefoníso méso tis tilefonítrias?

Do I have to dial '0' first? __ Πρέπει να πάρω πρώτα το μηδέν;
prépi na páro próta to midhén?

Do I have to book _____ Πρέπει να ζητήσω μια συνδιάλεξη;
my calls? *prépi na zitíso mya sindhiálexi?*

Could you dial this _____ Μπορείτε να μου πάρετε τον εξής αριθμό,
number for me, please? παρακαλώ;
*boríte na moo párete ton exís arithmó,
parakaló?*

Could you put me _____ Μπορείτε να με συνδέσετε με.../με το
through to.../extension..., εσωτερικό τηλέφωνο...;
please? *boríte na me sindhésete me.../me to
esoterikó tiléfono...?*

I'd like to place a _____ Θέλω να τηλεφωνήσω με έξοδα του
reverse-charge call to... δέκτη...
thélo na tilefoníso me éxodha too dhékti...

What's the charge per _____ Πόσο κάνει το λεπτό;
minute? *póso káni to leptó?*

Have there been any _____ Μου τηλεφώνησε κανείς;
calls for me? *moo tilefónise kanís?*

The conversation

Who is this, please? _____ Ποιός είναι;
pyos íne?

Hello, this is..._____ Γειά σας, είμαι ο/η...
Yásas, íme o/i...

Is this...? _____	Εσείς είστε ο/η...;
	esís íste o/i ...?
I'm sorry, I've dialled _____	Συγγνώμη, πήρα λάθος αριθμό
the wrong number	*sighnómi, píra láthos arithmó*
I can't hear you _____	Δε σας ακούω καλά
	dhe sas akóo-o kalá
I'd like to speak to... _____	Θα ήθελα να μιλήσω με το (ν)/τη (ν)...
	tha íthela na milíso me to(n)/ti(n)...
Is there anybody _____	Ξέρει κανείς αγγλικά;
who speaks English?	*xéri kanís angliká?*
Extension..., please_____	Μπορείτε να με συνδέσετε με το εσωτερικό
	τηλέφωνο...;
	boríte na me sindhésete me to esoterikó
	tiléfono...?
Could you ask him/her_____	Του/της λέτε να με πάρει τηλέφωνο;
to call me back?	*too/tis léte na me pári tiléfono?*
My name's... _____	Το όνομα μου είναι...Ο αριθμός τηλεφώνου
My number's...	είναι...
	to ónomámoo íne...o arithmós tilefónoo íne...
Could you tell him/her _____	Θέλετε να πείτε ότι τηλεφώνησα;
I called?	*thélete na píte óti tilefónisa?*
I'll call back tomorrow _____	Θα του/της ξανατηλεφωνήσω αύριο
	tha too/tis xanatilefoníso ávrio

Σας ζητούν στο τηλέφωνο _____	There's a phone call for you
Πρέπει να πάρετε πρώτα το μηδέν_____	You have to dial '0' first
'Ένα λεπτό, παρακαλώ _____	One moment, please
Δεν απαντά _____	There's no answer
Η γραμμή είναι κατειλημμένη_____	The line's engaged
Περιμένετε λιγάκι;_____	Do you want to hold?
Σας συνδέω τώρα _____	Putting you through
Πήρατε λάθος αριθμό _____	You've got a wrong number
Αυτή τη στιγμή λείπει ο/η... _____	He's/she's not here right now
Μπορείτε να του τηλεφωνήσετε... _____	He'll/she'll be back...
Αυτός είναι ο αυτόματος τηλεφωνητής __	This is the answering
του/της...	machine of...

Shopping

⑩ **S**hopping

● **Opening times:** in general shops are open on Mondays, Wednesdays and Saturdays from 8am until 2.30pm and on Tuesdays, Thursdays and Fridays from 8am to 1pm and from 5pm to 8pm. In tourist areas in the summer, however, most shops open every evening and stay open until late. In the big cities opening hours vary, and many shops remain open throughout the day.

αγορά market	κατάστημα αθλητικών ειδών sports shop	περίπτερο kiosk
ανθοπωλείο florist's	κατάστημα παιχνιδιών toy shop	πλυντήριο laundry
αρτοπωλείο (φούρνος) bakery	κατάστημα σουβενίρ souvenir shop	πολυκατάστημα department store
βιβλιοπωλείο bookshop	κοινόχρηστο πλυντήριο laundrette	πρακτορείο ταξιδιών travel agency
γαλακτοπωλείο dairy product shop	κομμωτήριο ladies' hairdresser's	ραφείο tailor's
γουναράδικο furrier's	κοσμηματοπωλείο jeweller's	σούπερ-μάρκετ supermarket
ζαχαροπλαστείο confectioner's (also acts as a café for its products)	κουρείο barber's shop	στεγνοκαθαριστήριο dry cleaner's
ινστιτούτο καλλονής beauty salon	κρεοπωλείο butcher's shop	τσαγκάρης cobbler's
ιχθυοπωλείο (ψαράδικο) fishmonger's	μανάβικο greengrocer's	υποδηματοπωλείο (παπουτσάδικο) shoe shop
καθαριστήριο cleaner's	μοδίστρια dressmaker's	φαρμακείο chemist's
καπελάδικο hat shop	οπτικός optician's	φωτογραφείο photographer's/ camera shop
καπνοπωλείο tobacconist's	παλαιοπωλείο antique shop	χαρτοπωλείο stationer's
	παντοπωλείο general store	ψιλικατζίδικο haberdasher's

⑩ .1 **S**hopping conversations

Where can I get...? _____	Σε ποιό κατάστημα μπορώ να βρω...; *se pyo katástima boró na vro...?*
When does this shop _____ open?	Τί ώρα ανοίγει αυτό το μαγαζί; *ti óra aníyi aftó to maghazi?*
Could you tell me _____ where the...department is?	Μπορείτε να μου πείτε πού είναι το τμήμα...; *boríte na moo píte poo íne to tmíma...?*
Could you help me, _____ please? I'm looking for...	Μπορείτε να με βοηθήσετε; Ψάχνω... *boríte na me voithísete? Psáchno...*
Do you sell English/ _____ American newspapers?	Πουλάτε αγγλικές/αμερικανικές εφημερίδες; *pooláte anglikés/amerikanikés efimerídhes?*

Σας εξυπηρετεί κανείς; _____ **Are you being served?**

No, I'd like... _____ Όχι. Θα ήθελα...
όhi. tha íthela...
I'm just looking, _____ Θα ρίξω μια ματιά, αν επιτρέπεται
  if that's all right *tha ríxo mya matyá, an epitrépete*

Τίποτ' άλλο; _____ **Anything else?**

Yes, I'd also like... _____ Ναι, θέλω και...
ne, thélo ke...
No, thank you. That's all ___ Όχι, ευχαριστώ. Τίποτ' άλλο
όhi, efcharistó. típotálo
Could you show me...? ____ Μπορείτε να μου δείξετε...
boríte na moo dhíxete
I'd prefer... _____ Προτιμώ...
protimó...
This is not what I'm _____ Δεν είναι αυτό που ψάχνω
  looking for *dhen íne aftó poo psáchno*
Thank you. I'll keep_____ Ευχαριστώ. Θα κοιτάξω και αλλού
  looking *efcharistó. tha kitáxo ke alóo*
Do you have _____ Μήπως έχετε κάτι που είναι...
  something...? *mípos éhete káti poo íne...*
– less expensive?_____ Μήπως έχετε κάτι πιο φτηνό;
mípos éhete káti pyo ftinó?
– something smaller?_____ Μήπως έχετε κάτι πιο μικρό;
mípos éhete káti pyo mikró?
– something larger? _____ Μήπως έχετε κάτι πιο μεγάλο;
mípos éhete káti pyo meghálo?
I'll take this one _____ Θα πάρω αυτό
tha páro aftó
Does it come with _____ Έχει οδηγίες χρήσεως μέσα;
  instructions? *éhi odhiyíes chríseos mésa?*
It's too expensive _____ Είναι πολύ ακριβό
íne polí akrivó
I'll give you... _____ Θα σας δώσω...
tha sas dhóso...
Could you keep this for ____ Μπορείτε να φυλάξετε αυτό για μένα; Θα
  me? I'll come back for it περάσω σε λίγο να το πάρω
  later *boríte na filáxete aftó ya ména? tha peráso*
se lígho na to páro
Have you got a bag _____ Μου δίνετε μία σακούλα, παρακαλώ;
  for me, please? *moo dhínete mya sakóola, parakaló?*
Could you giftwrap_____ Μπορείτε να το τυλίξετε για δώρο,
  it, please? παρακαλώ;
boríte na to tilíxete ya dhóro, parakaló?

Shopping

10

Λυπάμαι, δεν το έχουμε _____	I'm sorry, we don't have that
Λυπάμαι, μας έχει εξαντληθεί _____	I'm sorry, we're sold out
Λυπάμαι, θα το έχουμε πάλι... _____	I'm sorry, that won't be in until...
Μπορείτε να πληρώσετε στο ταμείο _____	You can pay at the cash desk
Δε δεχόμαστε πιστωτικές κάρτες _____	We don't accept credit cards
Δε δεχόμαστε ταξιδιωτικές επιταγές_____	We don't accept traveller's cheques
Δε δεχόμαστε ξένο συνάλλαγμα _____	We don't accept foreign currency

10 .2 Food

I'd like a hundred_____
grams of..., please
Θα ήθελα εκατό γραμμάρια ...
ha íthela ekató ghramárya...

– half a kilo of... _____
Θα ήθελα μισό κιλό...
tha íthela misó kiló...

– a kilo of... _____
Θα ήθελα ένα κιλό
tha íthela éna kiló...

Could you...it for me, _____
please?
Μπορείτε να μου το...:
boríte na moo to...

Could you slice it/ _____
dice it for me, please?
Μπορείτε να μου το κόψετε σε
φέτες/σε κομμάτια;
boríte na moo to kópsete se fétes/se komátya?

Could you grate it _____
for me, please?
Μπορείτε να μου το τρίψετε;
boríte na moo to trípsete?

Can I order it?_____
Μπορώ να το παραγγείλω;
boró na to paranghílo?

I'll pick it up tomorrow/ ____
at...
Θα περάσω αύριο/στις...να το πάρω
tha peráso ávrio/stis...na to páro

Can you eat/drink this? ____
Αυτό τρώγεται/πίνεται;
aftó tróyete/pínete?

What's in it? _____
Τί έχει μέσα;
ti éhi mésa?

10 .3 Clothing and shoes

I saw something in the ____
window. Shall I point it
out?
Είδα κάτι στη βιτρίνα. Να σας το δείξω;
ídha káti sti vitrína. na sas to dhíxo?

I'd like something to_____
go with this
Θέλω κάτι που να ταιριάζει μ' αυτό
thélo káti poo na teryázi maftó

Do you have shoes _____
to match this?
Έχετε ασορτί παπούτσια;
éhete asortí papóotsya?

I'm a size...in the UK_____
Στο Ηνωμένο Βασίλειο φοράω νούμερο...
sto inoméno vasílio foráo nóomero...

Can I try this on? _____
Μπορώ να το δοκιμάσω;
boró na to dhokimáso?

Where's the fitting room? __
Πού είναι το δοκιμαστήριο;
poo íne to dhokimastírio

It doesn't fit _____	Δε μου κάνει
	dhe moo káni
This is the right size _____	Αυτό είναι το σωστό νούμερο
	aftó íne to sostó nóomero
It doesn't suit me_____	Δε μου πάει
	dhe moo pái
Do you have this/ _____	Το έχετε και σε...;
these in...?	*to éhete ke se...?*
The heel's too high/low ____	Το τακόυνι είναι πολύ ψηλό/χαμηλό
	to takóoni íne polí psiló/chamiló
Is this/are these _____	Είναι αυτό/αυτά από γνήσιο δέρμα;
genuine leather?	*íne aftó/aftá apó ghnísyo dhérma?*
I'm looking for a... _____	Ψάχνω ένα...για ένα μωρό/παιδί...χρονών
for a...-year-old baby/child	*psáchno éna...ya éna moró/pedhí...chronón*
I'd like a...(made of)... _____	Θα ήθελα ένα...από...
	tha íthela éna...apó...
– silk _____	Θα ήθελα ένα...από μετάξι
	tha íthela éna...apó metáxi
– cotton _____	Θα ήθελα ένα...από βαμβάκι
	tha íthela éna...apó vamváki
– woollen _____	Θα ήθελα ένα...από μαλλί
	tha íthela éna...apó malí
– linen _____	Θα ήθελα ένα...από λινό
	tha íthela éna...apó linó
What temperature_____	Σε ποιά θερμοκρασία μπορώ να το πλύνω;
can I wash it at?	*se pya thermokrasía boró na to plíno?*
Will it shrink in the _____	Δε μαζεύει;
wash?	*dhe mazévi?*

Καθαριστήριο	Με το χέρι	Μην το στεγνώνετε
dry clean	by hand	στο στεγνωτήριο
Κρεμάστε το	Μη	do not tumble dry
υγρό	σιδερώνετε	Στο πλυντήριο
do no spin dry	do not iron	machine wash

At the cobbler's

Could you mend _____	Μπορείτε να φτιάξετε αυτά τα παπούτσια;
these shoes?	*boríte na ftyáxete aftá ta papóotsya?*
Could you put new _____	Μπορείτε να βάλετε καινούριες
soles/heels on these?	σόλες/καινούρια τακούνια σ΄ αυτά;
	boríte na válete kenóoryes sóles/kenóorya
	takóonya saftá?
When will they be _____	πότε θα είναι έτοιμα;
ready?	*póte tha íne étima?*
I'd like... _____	Θα ήθελα...
	tha íthela...
– a tin of shoe polish _____	Θα ήθελα ένα κουτάκι βερνίκι παπούτσιών
	tha íthela éna kootáki verníki papootsyón
– a pair of shoelaces_____	Θα ήθελα ένα ζευγάρι κορδόνια
	tha íthela éna zevghári kordhónya

I'd like a film for this_____
  camera, please — Θα ήθελα ένα φιλμ για αυτή τη μηχανή
  ha íthela éna film ya avtí ti mihaní
– a one twenty-six_____
  cartridge — Θα ήθελα μια κασέτα των 126
  tha íthela mya kaséta ton ekató íkosi éxl
– a slide film_____
  Θα ήθελα ένα φιλμ για σλάιτς
  tha íthela éna film ya slaidz
– a film cartridge_____
  Θα ήθελα μια κασέτα φιλμ
  tha íthela mya kaséta film
– a videotape_____
  Θα ήθελα μια βιντεοταινία
colour/black and white_____ tha íthela mya videotenía
  έγχρωμο/ασπρόμαυρο
super eight_____ énchromo/asprómavro
  σούπερ οχτώ
12/24/36 exposures_____ sóoper ochtó
  δωδεκάρι/εικοσιτεσσάρι/τριανταεξάρι
ASA/DIN number_____ dhodekári/ikositesári/triandaexári
  αριθμό ΑΣΑ
daylight film_____ arithmó asa
  φιλμ για κανονικό φως
film for artificial light_____ film ya kanonikó fos
  φιλμ για τεχνητό φως
Problems film ya technitó fos

Could you load the_____
  film for me, please? — Μπορείτε να βάλετε το φιλμ στη μηχανή,
  παρακαλώ;
Could you take the film____ boríte na válete to film sti michaní, parakaló
  out for me, please? — Μπορείτε να βγάλετε το φιλμ από τη
  μηχανή, παρακαλώ;
  boríte na vghálete to film apó ti michaní,
Should I replace_____ parakaló
  the batteries? — Πρέπει ν' αλλάξω τις μπαταρίες;
Could you have a look____ prépi naláxo tis bataríes?
  at my camera, please? — Μπορείτε να κοιτάξετε τη μηχανή μου; Δε
  It's not working λειτουργεί
The...is broken_____ boríte na kitáxete ti michanímoo? dhe litooryí
  Το...είναι χαλασμένο
The film's jammed_____ to...íne chalazméno
  Το φιλμ έχει μπλεχτεί
The film's broken_____ to film éhi blechtí
  Το φιλμ κόπηκε
The flash isn't working____ to film kópike
  Το φλας δε λειτουργεί
Processing and prints to flash dhe litooryí

I'd like to have this film____
  developed/printed, please — Θα ήθελα να εμφανίσετε/εκτυπώσετε αυτό
  το φιλμ
  tha íthela na emfanísete/ektipósete aftó to
I'd like...prints from_____ film
  each negative — Θα ήθελα...φωτογραφίες από κάθε αρνητικό
glossy/matt_____ tha íthela...fotgrafíes apó káthe arnitikó
  γυαλιστερό/ματ
  yalisteró/mat

6x9 _____	έξι επί εννιά
	éxi epí enyá
I'd like to reorder _____	Θέλω να παραγγείλω κι άλλες
these photos	φωτογραφίες απ' αυτές
	thélo na parangílo kyáles fotoghrafíes apaftés
I'd like to have this _____	Θα ήθελα να μου μεγεθύνετε αυτή τη
photo enlarged	φωτογραφία
	tha íthela na moo meyethínete aftí ti
How much is _____	fotoghrafía
processing?	Πόσο κάνει η εμφάνιση;
– printing _____	póso káni i emfánisi?
	Πόσο κάνει η εκτύπωση;
– it to re-order _____	póso káni i ektíposi?
	Πόσο κάνει η παραγγελία έξτρα
	φωτογραφιών;
– the enlargement _____	póso káni i paranghelía éxtra fotoghrafyón?
	Πόσο κάνει η μεγέθυνση;
When will they _____	póso káni i meyéthinsi?
be ready?	Πότε θα είναι έτοιμες;

🔟 .5 At the hairdresser's

Shopping

🔟

Do I have to make an _____	póte tha íne étimes?
appointment?	Πρέπει να κλείσω ραντεβού;
Can I come in straight _____	prépi na klíso randevóo?
away?	Μπορείτε να με εξυπηρετήσετε αμέσως;
How long will I have _____	boríte na me exipiritísete amésos?
to wait?	Πόση ώρα πρέπει να περιμένω;
I'd like a shampoo/ _____	pósi óra prépi na periméno?
haircut	Θα ήθελα να λούσετε/κόψετε τα μαλλιά
	μου
I'd like a shampoo for _____	tha íthela na lóosete/kópsete ta malyámoo
oily/dry hair, please	Θα ήθελα ένα σαμπουάν για λιπαρά/ξηρά
	μαλλιά
an anti-dandruff _____	tha íthela éna sampwán ya lipará/xirá malyá
shampoo	Θα ήθελα ένα σαμπουάν κατά της
	πιτυρίδας;
– a shampoo for _____	tha íthela éna sampwán katá tis pitirídhas
permed/coloured hair	Θα ήθελα ένα σαμπουάν για μαλλιά με
	περμανάντ/για βαμμένα μαλλιά
	tha íthela éna sampwán ya malyá me
– a colour rinse shampoo __	permanánt/ya vaména malyá
	Θα ήθελα ένα σαμπουάν με χρώμα
– a shampoo with _____	tha íthela éna sampwán me chróma
conditioner	Θα ήθελα ένα σαμπουάν με κρέμα
	λουσίματος
	tha íthela éna sampwán me kréma
– highlights _____	loosímatos
	Θα ήθελα ένα κουπ-σολέι
Do you have a colour _____	tha íthela éna koop-soléi
chart, please?	Έχετε ένα δειγματολόγιο χρωμάτων;
I want to keep it the _____	éhete éna dhighmatolóyio chromáton?
same colour	Θέλω να κρατήσω το ίδιο χρώμα
I'd like it darker/lighter ____	thélo na kratíso to ídhyo chróma
	Τα θέλω πιο σκούρα/πιο ανοιχτά
	ta thélo pyo skóora/pyo anichtá

I'd like a short fringe _____	Θέλω τη φράντζα μου πιο κοντή
	thélo ti frándza moo pyo kondí
Not too short at the back __	Θέλω να μην είναι πολύ κοντά πίσω
	thélo na min íne polí kondá píso
Not too long here _____	Θέλω να μην είναι πολύ μακριά εδώ
	thélo na min íne polí makriá edhó
I'd like/I don't want _____	(Δε) θέλω να έχω (πολλές) μπούκλες
(many) curls	*(dhe) thélo na écho (polés) bóokles*
It needs a little/_____	Τα θέλω λίγο πιο κοντά/πολύ πιο κοντά
a lot taken off	*ta thélo lígho pyo kondá /polí pyo kondá*
I want a completely _____	Θέλω τελείως διαφορετικό στυλ
different style	*thélo telíos dhiaforetikó stil*
I'd like it the same... _____	Θέλω τα μαλλιά μου σαν...
	thélo ta malyámoo san...
– as that lady's _____	Θέλω τα μαλλιά μου σαν αυτής της κυρίας
	thélo ta malyámoo san aftís tis kirías
– as in this photo_____	Θέλω τα μαλλιά μου όπως σ' αυτή τη φωτογραφία
	thélo ta malyámoo ópos saftí ti fotoghrafía
Could you put the _____	Μπορείτε να βάλετε την κάσκα πιο ψηλά/πιο χαμηλά;
drier up/down a bit?	*boríte na válete tingáska pyo psilá/pyo chamilá?*
I'd like a facial_____	Θα ήθελα μια μάσκα προσώπου
	tha íthela mya máska prosópoo
– a manicure _____	Θα ήθελα ένα μανικιούρ
	tha íthela éna manikyóor
– a massage _____	Θα ήθελα ένα μασάζ
	tha íthela éna masáz
Could you trim my..., _____	Μπορείτε να κόψετε λίγο...μου, παρακαλώ;
please?	*boríte na kópsete lígho...moo, parakaló?*
Could you trim _____	Μπορείτε να κόψετε λίγο τη φράντζα μου, παρακαλώ;
my fringe?	*boríte na kópsete lígho ti frándzamoo, parakaló?*
– my beard? _____	Μπορείτε να κόψετε λίγο τα γένια μου, παρακαλώ;
	boríte na kópsete lígho ta yényamoo, parakaló?
– my moustache? _____	Μπορείτε να κόψετε λίγο το μουστάκι μου, παρακαλώ;
	boríte na kópsete lígho to moostákimoo, parakaló?
I'd like a shave, please____	Ξύρισμα, παρακαλώ
	xírizma, parakaló
I'd like a wet shave, _____	Θέλω να με ξυρίσετε με ξυράφι, παρακαλώ
please	*thélo na me xirísete me xiráfi, parakaló*

Πώς θέλετε να κόψω τα μαλλιά σας; _____	How do you want it cut?
Πιο στυλ θέλετε; _____	What style did you have in mind?
Τί χρώμα θέλετε; _____	What colour did you want it?
Είναι καλή αυτή η θερμοκρασία; _____	Is the temperature all right for you?
Θέλετε κάτι να διαβάσετε; _____	Would you like something to read?
Θέλετε να πιείτε κάτι; _____	Would you like a drink?
Σας αρέσει έτσι; _____	Is this what you had in mind?

At the Tourist Information Centre

11 At the Tourist Information Centre

11 .1 Places of interest

Where's the Tourist Information Centre, please?	Πού βρίσκεται το γραφείο τουρισμού; *poo vrískete to grhafío toorizmóo?*
Do you have a city map?	Εχετε ένα χάρτη της πόλης; *éhete éna chárti tis pólis?*
Could you give me some information about...?	Μπορείτε να μου δώσετε πληροφορίες για... *boríte na moo dhósete plirofofíes ya ...*
How much is that?	Πόσο σας οφείλουμε; *póso sas ofíloome?*
What are the main places of interest?	Ποιά είναι τα σπουδαιότερα αξιοθέατα; *pya íne ta spoodheótera axiothéata?*
Could you point them out on the map?	Μπορείτε να τα δείξετε στο χάρτη; *boríte na ta dhíxete sto chárti?*
What do you recommend?	Τί μας συμβουλεύετε; *ti mas simvoolévete?*
We'll be here for a few hours	Θα μείνουμε εδώ λίγες ώρες *tha mínoome edhó líyes óres*
– a day	Θα μείνουμε εδώ μία μέρα *tha mínoome edhó mía méra*
– a week	Θα μείνουμε εδώ μία εβδομάδα *tha mínoome edhó mía evdhomádha*
We're interested in...	Ενδιαφερόμαστε για... *endhiaferómaste ya ...*
Is there a scenic walk around the city?	Μπορούμε να κάνουμε μια βόλτα στην πόλη; *boróome na kánoome mya vólta stimbóli?*
How long does it take?	Πόσο κρατάει; *póso kratái?*
Where does it start/end?	Πού είναι η αφετηρία/το τέρμα; *poo íne i afetiría/to térma?*
Are there any boat cruises here?	Υπάρχουν εδώ εκδρομικά καραβάκια; *ipárchoon edhó ekdhromiká karavákya?*
Where can we board?	Πού μπορούμε να μπαρκάρουμε; *poo boróome na barkároome?*
Are there any bus tours?	Γίνονται εκδρομές με πούλμαν; *yínonde ekdhromés me póolman?*
Where do we get on?	Πού πρέπει να ανεβούμε; *poo prépi na anevóome?*
Is there a guide who speaks English?	Υπάρχει ένας ξεναγός με αγγλικά; *ipárchi énas xenaghós me angliká?*
What trips can we take around the area?	Τί εκδρομές μπορεί να κάνει κανείς σ' αυτή την περιοχή; *ti ekdhromés borí na kánis saftí timberiohí?*
Are there any excursions?	Υπάρχουν οργανωμένες εκδρομές; *ipárchoon orghanoménes ekdhromés?*
Where do they go to?	Για πού; *ya poo?*
We'd like to go to...	Θέλουμε να πάμε σε... *théloome na páme se ...*
How long is the trip?	Πόσο κρατάει αυτή η διαδρομή; *póso kratái aftí i dhiadromí?*

English	Greek
How long do we _____ stay in...?	Πόση ώρα θα μείνουμε σε... *pósi óra tha mínoome se ...?*
Are there any guided _____ tours?	Γίνονται ξεναγήσεις εκεί; *yínonde xenayísis ekí?*
How much free time _____ will we have there?	Πόση ώρα θα έχουμε στη διάθεσή μας εκεί; *pósi óra tha échoome sti dhiáthesímas ekí?*
We want to go hiking _____	Θέλουμε να κάνουμε πεζοπορία *théloome na kánoome pezoporía*
Can we hire a guide? _____	Μπορούμε να νοικιάσουμε έναν ξεναγό; *boróome na nikyásoome énan xenaghó?*
Can I book mountain _____ huts?	Μπορώ να κλείσω ένα ορειβατικό καταφύγιο; *boró na klíso éna orivatikó katafíyo?*
What time does... _____ open/close?	Τί ώρα ανοίγει/κλείνει το...; *to óra aníyi/klíni to...?*
What days is...open/ _____ closed?	Ποιές μέρες είναι ανοιχτό/κλειστό το...; *pyes méres íne anichtó/klistó to ...?*
What's the admission _____ price?	Πόσο κοστίζει η είσοδος; *póso kostízi i ísodhos?*
Is there a group _____ discount?	Κάνετε έκπτωση για γκρουπ; *kánete ékptosi ya groop?*
Is there a child _____ discount?	Κάνετε έκπτωση για παιδιά; *kánete ékptosi ya pedhyá?*
Is there a discount_____ for pensioners?	Κάνετε έκπτωση για ηλικιωμένους; *kánete ékptosi ya ilikyoménoos?*
Can I take (flash) _____ photos/can I film here?	Επιτρέπεται εδώ η φωτογράφηση (με φλας)/η κινηματογράφηση; *epitrépete edhó i fotoghráfisi (me flash)/i kinimatoghráfisi?*
Do you have any _____ postcards of...?	Πουλάτε κάρτες με...; *pooláte kártes me ...?*
Do you have an _____ English...?	Εχετε ένα ... στα αγγλικά; *éhete éna ... sta angliká?*
– an English catalogue?____	Εχετε ένα κατάλογο στα αγγλικά; *éhete éna katálogho sta angliká?*
– an English programme?__	Εχετε ένα πρόγραμμα στα αγγλικά; *éhete éna prógrama sta angliká?*
– an English brochure? ____	Εχετε ένα φυλλάδιο στα αγγλικά; *éhete éna filádhio sta angliká?*

11 .2 Going out

● **In Greece theatres** and cinemas are usually open-air in the summer. Theatre performances usually start at 8.30pm in winter, but later in summer. Cinemas show films between approximately 1.30 and 11pm.

English	Greek
Do you have this _____ week's/month's entertainment guide?	Εχετε το Αθηνόραμα αυτής της εβδομάδας/αυτού του μήνα; *éhete to athinórama aftís tis evdhomádhas/aftóo too mína?*
What's on tonight? _____	Τί μπορούμε να κάνουμε απόψε; *ti boróome na kánoome apópse?*
We want to go to... _____	Θέλουμε να πάμε σε... *théloome na páme se ...*

Which films are showing?	Ποιές ταινίες παίζονται τώρα;	pyes teníes pézonde tóra?
What sort of film is that?	Τί είδος ταινία είναι αυτή;	ti ídhos tenía íne aftí?
suitable for the whole family	για όλες τις ηλικίες	ya óles tis ilikíes
not suitable for children	άνω των 12/16 χρονών	áno ton dhódheka me dekaéxi chronón
original version	πρωτότυπη έκδοση	protótipi ékdhosi
subtitled	με υπότιτλους	me ipotítloos
dubbed	ντουμπλαρισμένη	dooblarizméni
Is it a continuous showing?	Είναι παράσταση χωρίς διάλειμμα;	íne parástasi chorís dhiálima?
What's on at...?	Τί παίζουν στο...	ti pézoon sto...
– the theatre?	Τί παίζουν στο θέατρο;	ti pézoon sto théatro?
– the concert hall?	Τί παίζουν στην αίθουσα συναυλιών;	ti pézoon stin éthoosa sinavlyón?
– the opera?	Τί παίζουν στην όπερα;	ti pézoon stin ópera?
Where can I find a good disco around here?	Έχει εδώ κοντά καμμιά καλή ντίσκο;	éhi edhó kondá kamyá kalí dísko?
Is it members only?	Πρέπει να είσαι μέλος;	prépi na íse mélos?
Where can I find a good nightclub around here?	Έχει εδώ κοντά κανένα καλό νυχτερινό κέντρο;	éhi edhó kondá kanéna kaló nichterinó kéndro?
Is it evening wear only?	Είναι υποχρεωτική η βραδινή ενδυμασία;	íne ipochreotikí i vradhiní endhimasía?
Should I/we wear formal dress?	Ενδείκνυται η βραδινή ενδυμασία;	endhikníete i vradhiní endhimasía?
What time does the show start?	Τί ώρα αρχίζει η παράσταση;	ti óra archízi i parástasi?
When's the next soccer match?	Πότε θα γίνει ο επόμενος ποδοσφαιρικός αγώνας;	póte tha yíni o epómenos podhosferikós aghónas?
Who's playing?	Ποιές ομάδες παίζουν;	pyes omádhes pézoon?
I'd like an escort for tonight. Could you arrange that for me?	Θέλω για απόψε ένα/μία έσκορτ. Μπορείτε να μου το κανονίσετε;	thélo ya apópse éna/mía éskort. boríte na moo to kanonísete?

11

11 .3 **B**ooking tickets

Could you book some ____ tickets for us?	Μπορείτε να μας κλείσετε εισιτήρια; *boríte na mas klísete isitírya?*
We'd like to book... _____ seats/a table...	Θέλουμε...θέσεις/ένα τραπέζι *théloome...thésis/éna trapézi*
– in the stalls_____	Θέλουμε...θέσεις στην πλατεία *théloome...thésis stimblatía*
– on the balcony _____	Θέλουμε...θέσεις στον εξώστη *théloome...thésis ston exósti*
– box seats _____	Θέλουμε...θέσεις στο θεωρείο *théloome...thésis sto theorío*
– a table at the front _____	Θέλουμε...θέσεις/ένα τραπέζι μπροστά *théloome...thésis/éna trapézi brostá*
– in the middle_____	Θέλουμε...θέσεις/ένα τραπέζι στη μέση *théloome...thésis/éna trapézi sti mési*
– at the back _____	Θέλουμε...θέσεις/ένα τραπέζι πίσω *théloome...thésis/éna trapézi píso*
Could I book...seats for ____ the...o'clock performance?	Μπορώ να κλείσω...θέσεις για την παράσταση στις...; *boró na klíso...thésis ya timbarástasi stis...?*
Are there any seats left ____ for tonight?	Υπάρχουν ακόμα εισιτήρια για απόψε; *ipárchoon akóma isitírya ya apópse?*
How much is a ticket? _____	Πόσο κοστίζει το εισιτήριο; *póso kostízi to isitíryo?*
When can I pick the _____ tickets up?	Πότε μπορώ να πάρω τα εισιτήρια; *póte boró na páro ta isitírya?*
I've got a reservation _____	Έχω κλείσει θέσεις *écho klísi thésis*
My name's... _____	Το όνομά μου είναι... *to ónomámoo íne...*

Για ποιά παράσταση θέλετε να_____ κλείσετε εισιτήρια;	Which performance do you want to book for?
Πού θέλετε να καθίσετε;_____	Where would you like to sit?
Όλα πουλήθηκαν_____	Everything's sold out
Υπάρχουν μόνο θέσεις για όρθιους _____	It's standing room only
Υπάρχουν μόνο θέσεις στον εξώστη _____	We've only got balcony seats left
Υπάρχουν μόνο θέσεις στη γαλαρία _____	We've only got seats left in the gallery
Υπάρχουν μόνο θέσεις στην πλατεία_____	We've only got stalls seats left
Υπάρχουν μόνο θέσεις μπροστά _____	We've only got seats left at the front
Υπάρχουν μόνο θέσεις πίσω_____	We've only got seats left at the back
Πόσες θέσεις θέλετε; _____	How many seats would you like?
Πρέπει να πάρετε τα εισιτήρια πριν _____ από τις...	You'll have to pick up the tickets before...o'clock
Τα εισιτηριά σας, παρακαλώ_____	Tickets, please
Ορίστε, η θέση σας _____	This is your seat

Sports

Sports

.1 **S**porting questions

Where can we... _____ around here?	Πού μπορούμε να...εδώ; *poo boróome na...edhó?*
Is there a... _____ around here?	Υπάρχει ένα...εδώ κοντά; *ipárchi éna...edhó kondá?*
Can I hire a...here? _____	Μπορώ να νοικιάσω ένα...; *boró na nikyáso éna...?*
Can I take...lessons? _____	Γίνονται μαθήματα...; *yínonde mathímata...?*
How much is that per_____ hour/per day/a turn?	Πόσο κοστίζει την ώρα/τη μέρα/τη φορά; *póso kostízi tin óra/ti méra/ti forá?*
Do I need a permit _____ for that?	Χρειάζομαι μια άδεια για αυτό; *chriázome mya ádhya yavtó?*
Where can I get _____ the permit?	Πού μπορώ να βγάλω μια τέτοια άδεια; *poo boró na vghálo mya tétya ádhya?*

.2 **B**y the waterfront

Is it a long way to _____ the sea still?	Η θάλασσα είναι ακόμα μακριά; *i thálasa íne akóma makriá?*
Is there a...around here? ___	Υπάρχει κι ένα...εδώ κοντά; *ipárchi kyéna ... edhó kondá?*
– an outdoor/indoor/_____ public swimming pool	Υπάρχει και μια πισίνα εδώ κοντά; *ipárchi ke mya pisína edhó kondá?*
– a sandy beach_____	Υπάρχει και μια παραλία εδώ κοντά; *ipárchi ke mya paralía edhó kondá?*
– a nudist beach_____	Υπάρχει και μια πλαζ για γυμνιστές εδώ κοντά; *ipárchi ke mya plaz ya yimnistés edhó kondá?*
– mooring _____	Υπάρχει και μια μαρίνα εδώ κοντά; *ipárchi ke mya marína edhó kondá?*
Are there any rocks_____ here?	Έχει και βράχους εδώ; *éhi ke vráchoos edhó?*
When's high/low tide? ____	Τί ώρα έχει παλίρροια/άμπωτη; *ti óra éhi palíria/ámboti?*
What's the water _____ temperature?	Τί θερμοκρασία έχει το νερό; *ti thermokrasía éhi to neró?*
Is it (very) deep here? ____	Είναι (πολύ) βαθιά εδώ; *íne (polí) vathyá edhó?*
Can you stand here?_____	Πατώνεις εδώ; *patónis edhó?*
Is it safe (for children) _____ to swim here?	Είναι ασφαλές το κολύμπι εδώ (για παιδιά); *íne asfalés to kolímbi edhó (ya pedhyá)?*
Are there any currents? ___	Έχει ρεύματα εδώ; *éhi révmata edhó?*
Are there any rapids/ _____ waterfalls in this river?	Αυτό το ποτάμι έχει καταρράχτες; *aftó to potámi éhi kataráchtes?*
What does that flag/_____ buoy mean?	Τί σημαίνει εκείνη η σημαία/σημαδούρα εκεί; *ti siméni ekíni i siméa/simadhóora ekí?*

Is there a lifeguard _____ on duty here?	Έχει εδώ κανένα ακτοφύλακα που να προσέχει; *éhi edhó kanéna aktofílaka poo na proséhi?*
Are dogs allowed here? ___	Επιτρέπονται εδώ τα σκυλιά; *epitréponde edhó ta skilyá?*
Is camping on the _____ beach allowed?	Επιτρέπεται η κατασκήνωση εδώ στην παραλία; *epitrépete i kataskínosi edhó stimbaralía?*
Are we allowed to _____ build a fire here?	Επιτρέπεται να ανάβει κανείς εδώ φωτιά; *epitrépete nanávi kanís edhó fotyá?*

ΑΠΑΓΟΡΕΥΕΤΑΙ ΤΟ ΚΟΛΥΜΠΙ no swimming	ΑΠΑΓΟΡΕΥΕΤΑΙ ΤΟ ΨΑΡΕΜΑ no fishing	ΚΙΝΔΥΝΟΣ danger
ΑΠΑΓΟΡΕΥΕΤΑΙ ΤΟ ΣΕΡΦΙΝΓΚ no surfing	ΕΠΙΤΡΕΠΕΤΑΙ ΤΟ ΨΑΡΕΜΑ fishing permitted	ΜΟΝΟ ΜΕ ΑΔΕΙΑ permits only

12 .3 Water sports

Can I take water-ski _____ lessons here?	Μπορώ να κάνω εδώ θαλάσσιο σκι; *boró na káno edhó thalásyo ski?*
Can I get diving _____ instruction here?	Μπορώ να κάνω μαθήματα κατάδυσης; *boró na káno mathímata katadhísis?*
How large are the _____ groups?	Πόσο μεγάλα είναι τα γκρουπ; *póso meghála íne ta groop?*
What language _____ are the classes in?	Σε ποια γλώσσα παραδίνονται τα μαθήματα; *se pya ghlósa paradhínonde ta mathímata?*
Can I hire diving _____ equipment here?	Μπορώ να νοικιάσω εδώ εξαρτήματα κατάδυσης; *boró na nikyáso edhó exartímata katádhisis?*
Can I dive here? _____	Μπορώ να κάνω εδώ κατάδυση; *boró na káno edhó katádhisi?*

Sports

12

Sickness

13 **S**ickness

13 .1 **C**all (fetch) the doctor

Could you call/fetch a_____ doctor quickly, please?	Παρακαλώ, καλέστε/ειδοποιήστε γρήγορα ένα γιατρό *parakaló, kaléste/idhopiíste ghríghora éna yatró*
When does the doctor _____ have surgery?	Πότε δέχεται ο γιατρός; *póte dhéchete o yatrós?*
When can the doctor _____ come?	Πότε μπορεί να έρθει ο γιατρός; *póte borí na érthi o yatrós?*
I'd like to make an_____ appointment to see the doctor	Μπορείτε να μου κλείσετε ένα ραντεβού με το γιατρό; *boríte na moo klísete éna randevóo me to yatró?*
I've got an appointment ___ to see the doctor at...	Έχω ένα ραντεβού με το γιατρό στις... *écho éna randevóo me to yatró stis ...*
Which doctor/chemist _____ has night/weekend duty?	Ποιος γιατρός/ποιό φαρμακείο διανυκτερεύει/διανυκτερεύει το Σαββατοκύριακο; *pyos yatrós/pyo farmakío dhianikterévi/dhianikterévi to savatokíryako?*

13 .2 **P**atient's ailments

I don't feel well _____	Δεν αισθάνομαι καλά *dhen esthánome kalá*
I'm dizzy_____	Ζαλίζομαι *zalízome*
– ill_____	Είμαι άρρωστος/άρρωστη *íme árostos/árosti*
– sick_____	Ανακατεύεται το στομάχι μου *anakatévete to stomáchimoo*
I've got a cold_____	Είμαι κρυωμένος/κρυωμένη *íme krioménos/krioméni*
It hurts here _____	Πονάω εδώ *ponáo edhó*
I've been throwing up _____	Έκανα εμετό *ékana emetó*
I've got... _____	Μ' ενοχλεί... *menochlí...*
I'm running a _____ temperature of...degrees	Έχω...βαθμούς πυρετό *écho...vathmóos piretó*
I've been stung by_____ a wasp	Με τσίμπησε μια σφήκα *me tsíbise mya sfíka*
I've been stung by an_____ insect	Με τσίμπησε ένα έντομο *me tsíbise éna éndomo*
I've been bitten by _____ a dog	Με δάγκωσε ένας σκύλος *me dhángose énas skílos*
I've been stung by_____ a jellyfish	Με τσίμπησε μια μέδουσα; *me tsímbise mya medhóosa*
I've been bitten by _____ a snake	Με δάγκωσε ένα φίδι *me dhángose éna fídhi*

Sickness

13

I've been bitten by _____	Με δάγκωσε ένα ζώο
an animal	*me dhángose éna zó-o*
I've cut myself _____	Κόπηκα
	kópika
I've burned myself _____	Κάηκα
	káika
I've grazed myself _____	Γρατσουνίστηκα
	ghratsoonístika
I've had a fall _____	Έπεσα
	épesa
I've sprained my ankle ____	Στραμπούληξα τον αστράγαλό μου
	strambóolixa ton astrághalómoo
I've come for the _____	Έρχομαι για το μόρνιγκ-άφτερ-χάπι
morning-after pill	*érchome ya to morning-áfter-chápi*

.3 The consultation

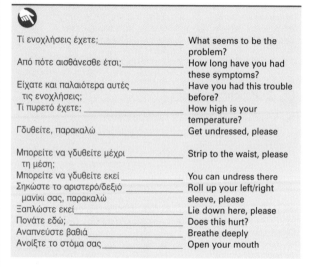

Τί ενοχλήσεις έχετε; _____	What seems to be the problem?
Από πότε αισθάνεσθε έτσι; _____	How long have you had these symptoms?
Είχατε και παλαιότερα αυτές _____ τις ενοχλήσεις;	Have you had this trouble before?
Τί πυρετό έχετε; _____	How high is your temperature?
Γδυθείτε, παρακαλώ _____	Get undressed, please
Μπορείτε να γδυθείτε μέχρι _____ τη μέση;	Strip to the waist, please
Μπορείτε να γδυθείτε εκεί _____	You can undress there
Σηκώστε το αριστερό/δεξιό _____ μανίκι σας, παρακαλώ	Roll up your left/right sleeve, please
Ξαπλώστε εκεί _____	Lie down here, please
Πονάτε εδώ; _____	Does this hurt?
Αναπνεύστε βαθιά _____	Breathe deeply
Ανοίξτε το στόμα σας _____	Open your mouth

Patient's medical history

I'm a diabetic _____	Είμαι διαβητικός
	íme dhiavitikós
I have a heart condition ____	Είμαι καρδιακός
	íme kardhiakós
I have asthma _____	Έχω άσθμα
	écho ásthma
I'm allergic to... _____	Είμαι αλλεργικός σε...
	íme aleryikós se...
I'm...months pregnant ____	Είμαι...μηνών έγκυος
	íme...minón éngios
I'm on a diet _____	Κάνω δίαιτα
	káno dhíeta

I'm on medication/the pill __ Παίρνω φάρμακα/το χάπι
pérno fármaka/to chápi

I've had a heart attack _____ Έχω ξαναπάθει καρδιακή προσβολή
once before *écho xanapáthi kardhiakí prosvolí*

I've had a(n)...operation ___ Έκανα εγχείρηση στο...
ékana enchírisi sto...

I've been ill recently _____ Πρόσφατα ήμουν άρρωστος/άρρωστη
prósfata ímoon árostos/árosti

I've got an ulcer_____ Έχω στομαχικό έλκος
écho stomachikó élkos

I've got my period_____ Έχω περίοδο
écho períodho

Είστε αλλεργικός σε κάτι; _____	Do you have any allergies?
Παίρνετε φάρμακα _____	Are you on any medication?
Κάνετε δίαιτα; _____	Are you on a diet?
Είστε έγκυος; _____	Are you pregnant?
Είστε εμβολιασμένος _____ κατά του τέτανου...;	Have you had a tetanus injection?

The diagnosis

Δεν είναι τίποτα σοβαρό_____	It's nothing serious
Έχετε σπάσει...το/τη...σας _____	Your...is broken
Έχετε στραμπουλήξει...το/τη...σας_____	You've got a strained/sprained...
Έχετε σκίσει...το/τη...σας _____	You've got (a) torn...
Έχετε μια φλεγμονή _____	You've got an inflammation
Έχετε σκωληκοειδίτιδα _____	You've got appendicitis
Έχετε βρογχίτιδα _____	You've got bronchitis
Έχετε ένα αφροδίσιο νόσημα _____	You've got a venereal disease
Έχετε γρίππη_____	You've got the flu
Πάθατε καρδιακή προσβολή _____	You've had a heart attack
Έχετε ίωση/βακτηριακή μόλυνση _____	You've got an infection (viral..., bacterial...)
Έχετε πνευμονία_____	You've got pneumonia
Έχετε έλκος _____	You've got an ulcer
Έχετε πάθει νευροκαβαλίκεμα _____	You've pulled a muscle
Έχετε κολπική μόλυνση _____	You've got a vaginal infection
Πάθατε τροφική δηλητηρίαση_____	You've got food poisoning
Έχετε πάθει ηλίαση_____	You've got sunstroke
Είστε αλλεργικός στο/στη... _____	You're allergic to...
Είστε έγκυος _____	You're pregnant
Θέλω να κάνω εξέταση του αίματός _____ σας/των ούρων σας/των κοπράνων σας	I'd like to have your blood/urine/stools tested

Πρέπει να ραφτεί _____	It needs stitching
Σας στέλνω σ' ένα ειδικό/σ' ένα _____ νοσοκομείο	I'm referring you to a specialist/sending you to hospital
Πρέπει να κάνουμε ακτινογραφίες _____	You'll need to have some x-rays taken
Πρέπει να περιμένετε δύο _____ λεπτά στην αίθουσα αναμονής	Could you wait in the waiting room, please?
Πρέπει να εγχειρισθείτε _____	You'll need an operation

Is it contagious? _____	Είναι κολλητικό; *íne kolitikó?*
How long do I have to _____ stay...?	Πόσο καιρό πρέπει να μείνω σε...; *póso kyeró prépi na míno se...?*
– in bed _____	Πόσο καιρό πρέπει να μείνω στο κρεβάτι; *póso kyeró prépi na míno sto kreváti?*
– in hospital _____	Πόσο καιρό πρέπει να μείνω στο νοσοκομείο; *póso kyeró prépi na míno sto nosokomío?*
Do I have to go on _____ a special diet?	Πρέπει να κάνω καμιά δίαιτα; *prépi na káno kamyá dhíeta?*
Am I allowed to travel? ____	Μπορώ να ταξιδέψω; *boró na taxidhépso?*
Can I make a new _____ appointment?	Μπορώ να κλείσω ένα άλλο ραντεβού; *boró na klíso éna álo randevóo?*
When do I have to _____ come back?	Πότε πρέπει να ξανάρθω; *póte prépi na xanártho?*
I'll come back _____ tomorrow	Θα ξανάρθω αύριο *tha xanártho ávrio*

Πρέπει να ξαναρθείτε αύριο/σε...μέρες ____	Come back tomorrow/in...days' time

🤚 .4 **M**edication and prescriptions

How do I take this _____ medicine?	Πώς πρέπει να το παίρνω αυτό το φάρμακο; *pos prépi na to pérno aftó to fármako?*
How many capsules/ _____ drops/injections/spoonfuls/ tablets each time?	Πόσες κάψουλες/σταγόνες/ενέσεις/πόσα κουταλάκια/χάπια τη φορά; *póses kapsóoles/staghónes/enésis/pósa kootalákya/chápya ti forá?*
How many times a day? ___	Πόσες φορές την ημέρα; *póses forés tin iméra?*
I've forgotten my _____ medication. At home I take...	Ξέχασα τα φάρμακά μου. Σπίτι χρησιμοποιώ... *xéchasa ta fármakámoo. spíti chrisimopió ...*
Could you make out a _____ prescription for me?	Μπορείτε να μου δώσετε μια συνταγή; *boríte na moo dhósete mya sintayí?*

Θα σας δώσω αντιβιοτικά/ένα σιρόπι/ ___ ένα ηρεμιστικό/ένα παυσίπονο	I'm prescribing antibiotics/a mixture/a tranquillizer/painkillers
Πρέπει να ξεκουραστείτε ___	Have lots of rest
Καλύτερα να μην βγείτε έξω ___	Stay indoors
Πρέπει να μείνετε στο κρεβάτι ___	Stay in bed

αλείφω rub on	κατά τη διάρκεια... ημερών	παίρνω take
αλοιφή ointment	for...days	πριν από κάθε γεύμα
αυτά τα φάρμακα επηρεάζουν την ικανότητα οδήγησης this medication impairs your driving	καταπίνω ολόκληρο swallow whole κάψουλες capsules κουτάλια/κουταλάκια spoonfuls	before every meal σταγόνες drops τελειώνω τη θεραπεία finish the course
διαλύω σε νερό dissolve in water	(tablespoons/ teaspoons)	of treatment ...φορές το μερόνυχτο
ενέσεις injections κάθε...ώρες every...hours	μόνο για εξωτερική χρήση not for internal use	...times a day χάπια pills

🔞 .5 At the dentist's

Do you know a good ___ dentist?	Ξέρετε ένα καλό οδοντογιατρό; *xérete éna kaló odhondoyatró?*
Could you make a ___ dentist's appointment for me? It's urgent	Μπορείτε να μου κλείσετε ραντεβού με τον οδοντογιατρό; Είναι επείγον *boríte na moo klísete randevóo me ton odhondoyatró? íne epíghon*
Can I come in today, ___ please?	Μπορώ να έρθω σήμερα, παρακαλώ; *boró na értho símera, parakaló?*
I have (terrible) ___ toothache	Έχω (φοβερό) πονόδοντο *écho (foveró) ponódhondo*
Could you prescribe/ ___ give me a painkiller?	Μπορείτε να μου γράψετε/δώσετε ένα παυσίπονο; *boríte na moo ghrápsete/dhósete éna pafsípono?*
A piece of my tooth ___ has broken off	Έσπασε ένα κομματάκι του δοντιού μου/του τραπεζίτη μου *éspase éna komatáki too dondyóomoo/too trapezítimoo*
My filling's come out ___	Βγήκε ένα σφράγισμα *vyíke éna sfráyizma*
I've got a broken crown ___	Έσπασε η κορόνα μου *éspase i koróna moo*
I'd like/I don't want a ___ local anaesthetic	Θέλω/δε θέλω τοπική αναισθησία *thélo/dhe thélo topikí anesthisía*

Can you do a makeshift___ repair job?	Μπορείτε να με βοηθήσετε προσωρινά;
	boríte na me voithísete prosoriná?
I don't want this tooth ____ pulled	Δε θέλω να το βγάλετε αυτόν τον τραπεζίτη
	dhe thélo na to vghálete aftón ton trapezíti
My dentures are broken.___ Can you fix them?	Η μασέλα μου έσπασε. Μπορείτε να τη φτιάξετε;
	i masélamoo éspase. boríte na ti ftyáxete?

Ποιό δόντι/ποιός τραπεζίτης σας _____ πονάει;	Which tooth/molar hurts?
Έχετε ένα απόστημα _____	You've got an abscess
Πρέπει να κάνω απονεύρωση_____	I'll have to do a root canal
Θα σας κάνω τοπική αναισθησία _____	I'm giving you a local anaesthetic
Πρέπει να βουλώσω/βγάλω/λιμάρω_____ αυτό το δόντι	I'll have to fill/pull/file this tooth down
Πρέπει να τρυπήσω το δόντι _____	I'll have to drill
Ανοίξτε το στόμα _____	Open wide, please
Κλείστε το στόμα _____	Close your mouth, please
Ξεπλύντε το _____	Rinse, please
Πονάει ακόμα; _____	Does it hurt still?

Sickness

13

In trouble

14 In trouble

14.1 Asking for help

Help! _____	Βοήθεια! *voíthya!*
Fire! _____	Φωτιά! *fotyá!*
Police! _____	Αστυνομία! *astinomía!*
Quick! _____	Γρήγορα! *ghríghora!*
Danger! _____	Κίνδυνος! *kíndhinos!*
Watch out! _____	Προσοχή! *prosohí!*
Stop! _____	Σταματήστε! *stamatíste!*
Be careful! _____	Προσοχή! *prosohí!*
Don't! _____	Μή! *mi!*
Let go! _____	Άφήστέ το! *afiséto*
Stop that thief! _____	Πιάστε τον κλέφτη! *pyáste tongléfti!*
Could you help me, _____ please?	Μπορείτε να με βοηθήσετε; *boríte na me voithísete?*
Where's the police _____ station/emergency exit/fire escape?	Πού είναι το αστυνομικό τμήμα/η έξοδος κινδύνου/η σκάλα πυρκαγιάς; *poo íne to astinomikó tmíma/i éxodhos kindhínoo/i skála pirkayás?*
Where's the nearest fire ___ extinguisher?	Πού βρίσκεται ένας πυροσβεστήρας; *poo vrískete énas pirosvestíras?*
Call the fire brigade! _____	Ειδοποιείστε την πυροσβεστική υπηρεσία! *idhopiíste timbirosvestikí ipiresía!*
Call the police! _____	Τηλεφωνήστε στην αστυνομία! *tilefoníste stin astinomía!*
Call an ambulance! _____	Ειδοποιήστε ένα ασθενοφόρο! *idhopiíste éna asthenofóro!*
Where's the nearest _____ phone?	Πού υπάρχει ένα τηλέφωνο; *poo ipárchi éna tiléfono?*
Could I use your phone? ___	Μπορώ να χρησιμοποιήσω το τηλέφωνό σας; *boró na chrisimopiíso to tiléfonósas?*
What's the emergency _____ number?	Ποιός είναι ο αριθμός του συναγερμού; *pyos íne o arithmós too sinayermóo?*
What's the number for _____ the police?	Ποιός είναι ο αριθμός της αστυνομίας; *pyos íne o arithmós tis astinomías?*

In trouble

14

14 .2 Loss

I've lost my purse/_____ wallet	Έχασα το πορτοφόλι μου *échasa to portofólimoo*
I lost my...yesterday _____	Ξέχασα χτες το...μου *xéchasa chtes to...moo*
I left my...here _____	Άφησα εδώ το...μου *áfisa edhó to...moo*
Did you find my...? _____	Μήπως βρήκατε το...μου; *mípos vríkate to...moo?*
It was right here_____	Ήταν εδώ *tan edhó*
It's quite valuable _____	Είναι πολύτιμο *íne polítimo*
Where's the lost_____ property office?	Πού βρίσκεται το γραφείο ευρεθέντων αντικειμένων; *poo vrískete to ghrafío evrethéndon andikiménon?*

14 .3 Accidents

There's been an accident __	Έγινε ένα ατύχημα *éyine éna atíhima*
Someone's fallen into _____ the water	Κάποιος έπεσε στο νερό *kápyos épese sto neró*
There's a fire_____	Ξέσπασε πυρκαγιά *xéspase pirkayá*
Is anyone hurt? _____	Υπάρχουν τραυματίες; *ipárchoon travmatíes?*
Some people have _____ been/no one's been injured	(Δεν) υπάρχουν τραυματίες *(dhen) ipárchoon travmatíes*
There's someone in _____ the car/train still	Έχει και άλλον έναν στο αυτοκίνητο/στο τρένο *éhi ke álo énan sto aftokínito/sto tréno*
It's not too bad. Don't_____ worry	Δεν είναι και τόσο άσχημα. Μην ανησυχείτε *dhen íne ke tóso áschima. min anisihíte*
Leave everything the _____ way it is, please	Μην κουνήσετε τίποτα *min koonísete típota*
I want to talk to the_____ police first	Θέλω πρώτα να μιλήσω με την αστυνομία *thélo próta na milíso me tin astinomía*
I want to take a _____ photo first	Θέλω πρώτα να βγάλω μία φωτογραφία *thélo próta na vghálo mya fotoghrafía*
Here's my name_____ and address	Να το όνομά μου και η διεύθυνσή μου *na to ónomámoo ke i dhiéfthinsímoo*
Could I have your _____ name and address?	Μου δίνετε το όνομά σας και τη διεύθυνσή σας; *moo dhínete to ónomásas ke ti dhiéfthinsísas?*
Could I see some_____ identification/your insurance papers?	Μπορώ να δω την ταυτότητά σας/τα χαρτιά της ασφάλειάς σας; *boró na dho tin taftótitásas/ta chartyá tis asfalyás sas?*
Will you act as a _____ witness?	Θέλετε να εμφανιστείτε ως μάρτυρας; *thélete na emfanistíte os mártiras?*
I need the details for _____ the insurance	Χρειάζομαι τα στοιχεία για την ασφάλεια *chriázome ta stihía ya tin asfálya*

Are you insured?	Είστε ασφαλισμένος/ασφαλισμένη;
	íste asfalizménos/asfalizméni?
Third party or comprehensive?	Απλή ή μικτή ασφάλεια;
	aplí i miktí asfálya?
Could you sign here, please?	Παρακαλώ, να υπογράψετε εδώ
	parakaló, na ipoghrápsete edhó

14 .4 Theft

I've been robbed	Μ' έκλεψαν
	méklepsan
My...has been stolen	Έκλεψαν το...μου
	éklepsan to...moo
My car's been broken into	Παραβίασαν το αυτοκίνητό μου
	paravíasan to aftokínitómoo

14 .5 Missing person

I've lost my child/grandmother	Έχασα το παιδί μου/τη γιαγιά μου
	échasa to pedhímoo/ti yayámoo
Could you help me find him/her?	Μπορείτε να με βοηθήσετε να το/τη βρω;
	boríte na me voithísete na to/ti vro?
Have you seen a small child?	Μήπως είδατε ένα μικρό παιδί;
	mípos ídhate éna mikró pedhí?
He's/she's...years old	Είναι...χρονών
	íne...chronó
He's/she's got short/long/blond/red/brown/black/grey/curly/straight/frizzy hair	Έχει...κοντά/μακριά/ξανθά/κόκκινα/καστανά/μαύρα/γκρίζα/σγουρά/ίσια/κατσαρά μαλλιά
	éhi kondá/makryá/xanthá/kókina/kastaná/mávra/gríza/zghoorá/ísya/ katsará malyá
with a ponytail	με αλογοουρά
	me aloghó-oorá
with plaits	με κοτσίδες
	me kotsídhes
in a bun	με κότσο
	me kótso
He's/she's got blue/brown/green eyes	Τα μάτια του/της είναι μπλε/καστανά/πράσινα
	ta mátya too/tis íne ble/kastaná/prásina
He's wearing swimming trunks/mountaineering boots	Φοράει μαγιό/παπούτσια ορειβασίας
	forái mayó/papóotsya orivasías
with/without glasses/a bag	με/χωρίς γυαλιά/τσάντα
	me/chorís yalyá/tsánda
tall/short	ψηλός/κοντός
	psilós/kondós
This is a photo of him/her	Να μια φωτογραφία του/της
	na mya fotoghrafía too/tis
He/she must be lost	Μάλλον έχασε το δρόμο
	málon échase to dhrómo

An arrest

Τα χαρτιά του αυτοκινήτου σας, _____ παρακαλώ	Your registration papers, please
Τρέχατε πολύ _____	You were speeding
Παρκάρατε παράνομα _____	You're not allowed to park here
Δε βάλατε λεφτά στο παρκόμετρο _____	You haven't put money in the meter
Τα φώτα σας δε λειτουργούν _____	Your lights aren't working
Θα πληρώσετε πρόστιμο ... δραχμών _____	That's a...drachma fine
Θέλετε να πληρώσετε αμέσως; _____	Do you want to pay on the spot?
Πρέπει να πληρώσετε αμέσως _____	You'll have to pay on the spot

I don't speak Greek _____	Δε μιλάω ελληνικά
	dhe miláo eliniká
I didn't see the sign _____	Δεν είδα εκείνη την πινακίδα
	dhen ídha ekíni timbinakídha
I don't understand _____ what it says	Δεν καταλαβαίνω τι λέει εδώ
	dhengkatalavéno ti léi edhó
I was only doing... _____ kilometres an hour	Οδηγούσα μόνο ... χιλιόμετρα την ώρα
	odhighóosa móno ... hilyómetra tin óra
I'll have my car checked ___	Θα πάω το αυτοκίνητό μου στο συνεργείο
	tha páo to aftokínitómoo sto sineryío
I was blinded by _____ oncoming lights	Τυφλώθηκα από ένα αυτοκίνητο που ερχόταν από την αντίθετη κατεύθυνση
	tiflóthika apó éna aftokínito poo erchótan apó tin andítheti katéfthinsi

At the police station

I want to report a _____ collision/missing person/rape	Ήρθα για να αναφέρω μια σύγκρουση/μια απώλεια/ένα βιασμό
	írtha ya na anaféro mya síngroosi/mya apólya/éna viazmó
Could you make out _____ a report, please?	Μπορείτε να κάνετε αναφορά για το αυτόφωρο;
	boríte na kánete anaforá ya to aftóforo?
Could I have a copy _____ for the insurance?	Μπορείτε να μου δώσετε ένα αντίγραφο για την ασφάλεια;
	boríte na moo dhósete éna andíghrafo ya tin asfálya?
I've lost everything _____	Έχασα τα πάντα
	échasa ta pánda
I've no money; I don't _____ know what to do	Τα λεφτά μου τελείωσαν, δεν ξέρω τί να κάνω
	ta leftámoo telíosan, dhengxéro ti na káno
Could you lend me a _____ little cash?	Μπορείτε να μου δανείσετε λίγα λεφτά;
	boríte na moo dhanísete lígha leftá?

In trouble

14

Greek	English
Πού έγινε αυτό; _____	Where did it happen?
Τί χάσατε; _____	What's missing?
Τί έκλεψαν; _____	What's been taken?
Δώστε μου την ταυτότητά σας, _____ παρακαλώ	Could I see some identification?
Τί ώρα έγινε; _____	What time did it happen?
Ποιοί ήταν μπλεγμένοι σ' αυτό; _____	Who was involved?
Υπάρχουν μάρτυρες; _____	Are there any witnesses?
Να συμπληρώσετε αυτό, παρακαλώ _____	Fill this out, please
Υπογράψτε εδώ, παρακαλώ _____	Sign here, please
Θέλετε ένα διερμηνέα; _____	Do you want an interpreter?

I'd like an interpreter _____ Θα ήθελα ένα διερμηνέα
tha íthela éna dhierminéa

I'm innocent _____ Είμαι αθώος
íme athó-os

I don't know anything _____ Δεν ξέρω τίποτα για αυτό
about it *dhengxéro típota yaftó*

I want to speak to _____ Θέλω να μιλήσω με κάποιον από ...
someone from... *thélo na milíso me kápyon apó ...*

I want to speak to _____ Θέλω να μιλήσω με κάποιον από το
someone from the British βρεττανικό προξενείο
consulate *thélo na milíso me kápyon apó to vretanikó proxenío*

I need to see someone _____ Θέλω να μιλήσω με κάποιον από τη
from the British embassy βρεττανική πρεσβεία
thélo na milíso me kápyon apó ti vretanikí prezvía

I want a lawyer who _____ Θέλω ένα δικηγόρο που να μιλάει αγγλικά
speaks English *thélo éna dhikighóro poo na milái angliká*

Word list

Word list English - Greek

● **This word list** is intended to supplement the previous chapters. Nouns are usually accompanied by the Greek definite article in order to indicate whether the word is masculine (ο), feminine (η), or neuter (το). In the case of a plural noun the form of the definite article will be οι for masculine and feminine nouns and τα for neuter nouns.

In a number of cases, words not contained in this list can be found elsewhere in this book, namely alongside the diagrams of the car, the bicycle and the tent. Many food terms can be found in the Greek-English list in 4.7.

A

a little	λίγο	lígho
about	περίπου	perípoo
above	πάνω	páno
abroad	το εξωτερικό	to exoterikó
accident	το ατύχημα	to atíhima
according	κατά	katá
adder	η οχιά	i ochyá
addition	η πρόσθεση	i prósthesi
address	η διεύθυνση	i dhiéfthinsi
admission	η είσοδος	i ísodhos
admission price	η είσοδος	i ísodhos
adult	μεγάλος	meghálos
advice	η συμβουλή	i simvoolí
afraid (I am)	φοβάμαι	fováme
after, afterwards	μετά	metá
aftershave	το άφτερ-σέιβ	to áfter-séiv
afternoon	το απόγευμα	to apóyevma
again	ξανά	xaná
against	ενάντια σε	enándya se
age	η ηλικία	i ilikía
AIDS	ΕΙΤΖ	éitz
air mattress	το αερόστρωμα	to aeróstroma
air-conditioning	ο κλιματισμός	o klimatizmós
aircraft	το αεροπλάνο	to aeropláno
airport	το αεροδρόμιο	to aerodhrómio
airsickness bag	η σακούλα για εμετό	i sakóola ya emetó
alarm	ο συναγερμός	o sinayermós
alarm clock	το ξυπνητήρι	to xipnitíri
alcohol	το αλκοόλ	to alkoól
allergic	αλλεργικός	aleryikós
alone/only	μόνος	mónos
alter	αλλάζω	alázo
always	πάντα	pánda
ambulance	το ασθενοφόρο	to asthenofóro
amount	το ποσό	to posó
amusement park	το λούνα παρκ	to lóonapark
anaesthetize	ναρκώνω	narkóno
anchovy	η αντσούγια	i antsóoya
ancient/very old	αρχαίος	archéos
angry	θυμωμένος	thimoménos
animal	το ζώο	to zóo
ankle	ο αστράγαλος	o astrághalos
answer	η απάντηση	i apándisi
ant	το μυρμήγκι	to mirmíngi

antibiotics	τα αντιβιοτικά	*ta andiviotiká*
antifreeze	το αντιψυκτικό	*to andipsiktikó*
antique (an)	η αντίκα	*i antíka*
anus	ο πρωκτός	*o proktós*
apartment	το διαμέρισμα	*to dhiamérizma*
apologies	συγγνώμη	*sighnómi*
appetiser	το ορεκτικό	*to orektikó*
apple juice	ο χυμός μήλων	*o himós mílon*
apple	το μήλο	*to mílo*
apple sauce	ο πολτός μήλων	*o poltós mílon*
apple pie	η μηλόπιτα	*i milópita*
appointment/date	το ραντεβού	*to randevóo*
apricot	το βερίκοκο	*to veríkoko*
April	ο Απρίλιος	*o aprílios*
archbishop	ο αρχιεπίσκοπος	*o archiepískopos*
architecture	η αρχιτεκτονική	*i architektonikí*
arm	το χέρι	*to héri*
arrive	φτάνω	*ftáno*
arrow	το βέλος	*to vélos*
art	η τέχνη	*i téchni*
artery	η αρτηρία	*i artiría*
artichokes	οι αγγινάρες	*i angináres*
artificial repiration	η τεχνητή αναπνοή	*i technití anapnoí*
ashtray	το τασάκι	*to tasáki*
ask (for)	ζητώ	*zitó*
ask (question)	ρωτάω	*rotáo*
asparagus	τα σπαράγγια	*ta sparángya*
aspirin	η ασπιρίνη	*i aspiríni*
at home	σπίτι	*spíti*
aubergine	η μελιτζάνα	*i melitzána*
August	ο Αύγουστος	*o ávghoostos*
automatic (adj.)	αυτόματος	*aftómatos*
automatic (noun)	το αυτόματο	*to aftómato*
autumn	το φθινόπωρο	*to fthinóporo*
awake	ξύπνιος	*xípnios*
awning	το αλεξήλιο	*to alexílyo*

B

baby food	το φαγητό για μωρά	*to fayitó ya morá*
baby	το μωρό	*to moró*
baby's bottle	το μπιμπερό	*to biberó*
babysitter	η μπέιμπυ σίτερ	*i béibi-síter*
bachelor	ο εργένης	*o eryénis*
back	η πλάτη	*i pláti*
back, at the	πίσω	*píso*
backpack	ο σάκος	*o sákos*
bacterial infection	η βακτηριακή μόλυνση	*i vaktiriakí mólinsi*
bad (serious)	σοβαρός	*sovarós*
bad	κακός	*kakós*
bakery	το αρτοπωλείο/ο φούρνος	*to artopolío/o fóornos*
balcony (in theatre)	ο εξώστης	*o exóstis*
balcony	το μπαλκόνι	*to balkóni*
ball	η μπάλα	*i bála*
ballet	το μπαλέτο	*to baléto*
banana	η μπανάνα	*i banána*
bandage	ο επίδεσμος	*o epídhezmos*

Word list

15

bank	η τράπεζα	i trápeza
bank card	η τραπεζική κάρτα	i trapezikí kárta
bank (river)	η όχθη	i óchthi
bar (café)	το μπαρ	to bar
bar (drink's cabinet)	το μπαρ	to bar
barbecue	το μπαρμπεκιού	to barbekyóo
barber	ο κουρέας	o kooréas
basketball	το μπάσκετ	to básket
bath/swim	το μπάνιο	to bányo
bath foam	το αφρόλουτρο μπάνιου	to afrólootro bányoo
bath	το μπάνιο	to bányo
bath towel	η πετσέτα	i petséta
bathing cap	η σκούφια του μπάνιου	i skóofya too bányoo
bathing-hut	η καμπίνα	i kabína
battery	η μπαταρία	i bataría
beach	η πλαζ	i plaz
beans	τα φασόλια	ta fasólya
beautiful	όμορφος	ómorfos
beauty parlour	το ινστιτούτο καλλονής	to institóoto kalonís
bed	το κρεβάτι	to kreváti
bee	η μέλισσα	i mélissa
beef	το βοδινό κρέας	to vodhinó kréas
beer	η μπύρα	i bíra
beetroot	το παντζάρι	to padzári
begin	αρχίζω	archízo
beginner	ο αρχάριος	o archáryos
behind	πίσω από	píso apó
belly	η κοιλιά	i kilyá
belly ache	ο κοιλόπονος	o kilóponos
beloved	αγαπημένος	aghapiménos
belt	η ζώνη	i zóni
bicarbonate of soda	η σόδα	i sódha
bicycle	το ποδήλατο	to podhílato
bicycle pump	η τρόμπα	i trómba
big	μεγάλος	meghálos
bikini	το μπικίνι	to bikíni
bill	ο λογαριασμός	o loghariazmós
billiards	το μπιλιάρδο	to bilyárdho
biro	το στυλό	to stiló
birthday	τα γενέθλια	ta yenéthlia
birthday (it's my)	έχω γενέθλια	écho yenéthlia
biscuits	τα μπισκότα	ta biskóta
bite (verb)	δαγκώνω	dhangóno
bitter (adj.)	πικρός	pikrós
black	μαύρος	mávros
black bread	το μαύρο ψωμί	to mávro psomí
bland	άνοστος	ánostos
blanket	η κουβέρτα	i koovérta
bleach	ξανθαίνω	xanthéno
blister	η φουσκάλα	i fooskála
block of flats	η πολυκατοικία	i polikatikía
blond	ξανθός	xanthós
blood	το αίμα	to éma
blood pressure	η αρτηριακή πίεση	i artiriakí píesi

blouse	η μπλούζα	i blóoza
blow-dry hair	στεγνώνω τα μαλλιά	steghnóno ta malyá
blue	μπλε	ble
boat	το καράβι	to karávi
body lotion	η λοσιόν	i losyón
body	το σώμα	to sóma
boiled	βρασμένος	vrazménos
bone	το κόκαλο	to kókalo
bonnet	το καπό	to kapó
book	το βιβλίο	to vivlío
book (verb)	κλείνω	klíno
bookshop	το βιβλιοπωλείο	to vivliopolío
booked	κρατημένος	kratiménos
borders (of country)	τα σύνορα	ta sínora
bored, I am	βαριέμαι	varyéme
boring	πληκτικός	pliktikós
born	γεννημένος	yeniménos
borrow	δανείζομαι	dhanízome
boss	το αφεντικό	to afendikó
botanical gardens	ο βοτανικός κήπος	o votanikós kípos
both	και οι δύο/και τα δύο	ke i dhío/ke ta dhío
bothers me	μ' ενοχλεί	menochlí
bottle	το μπουκάλι	to bookáli
box (theatre)	το θεωρείο	to theorío
box	το κουτί	to kootí
boy	το αγόρι	to aghóri
bra	το σουτιέν	to sootyén
bracelet	το βραχιόλι	to vrahyóli
braised	βρασμένος	vrazménos
brake	το φρένο	to fréno
brake fluid	το υγρό φρένου	to ighró frénoo
brake oil	το λάδι φρένου	to ládhi frénoo
brandy	το κονιάκ	to konyák
bread	το ψωμί	to psomí
bread-roll	το ψωμάκι	to psomáki
break	σπάζω	spázo
breakfast	το πρωινό	to proinó
breast	το στήθος	to stíthos
bridge	η γέφυρα	i yéfira
briefs	το σλιπάκι	to slipáki
bring	φέρνω	férno
brochure	το φυλλάδιο	to filádhyo
broken	σπασμένος, χαλασμένος	spazménos, chalazménos
broth	το ζουμί	to zoomí
brother	ο αδερφός	o adherfós
brown	καστανός	kastanós
brush	η βούρτσα	i vóortsa
Brussels sprouts	λαχανάκια Βρυξελλών	lachanákya vrixelón
bucket	ο κουβάς	o koovás
bugs	τα ζωύφια	ta zoífya
building	το κτίριο	to ktíryo
buoy	η σημαδούρα	i simadhóora
bureau de change	το γραφείο συναλλάγματος	to ghrafío sinalághmatos
burglary	η διάρρηξη	i dhiárixi

15

burn	το έγκαυμα	to éngkavma
burn (verb)	καίω	kéo
burnt	καμένος	kaménos
bus stop	η στάση	i stási
bus station	ο σταθμός λεωφορείων	o stathmós leoforíon
bus	το λεωφορείο	to leoforío
business class	μπιζνεσκλάς	biznesklás
business trip	η περιοδεία	i perodhía
butane gas	το υγραέριο	to ighraério
butcher	ο χασάπης	o chasápis
butter	το βούτυρο	to vóotiro
button	το κουμπί	to koobí
buy	αγοράζω	aghorázo
by phone	τηλεφωνικώς	tilefonikós
by air	αεροπορικώς	aeroporikós

C

cabbage	το λάχανο	to láchano
cabin	η καμπίνα	i kabína
café	το καφενείο	to kafenío
cake	η πάστα, η τούρτα	i pásta, i tóorta
call (phone)	τηλεφωνώ	tilefonó
camera	η φωτογραφική μηχανή	i fotghrafikí michaní
camp (verb)	κατασκηνώνω	kataskinóno
camp site	το κάμπινγκ	to kámping
camping van	το κάμπερ	to kámper
camping permit	η άδεια κατασκήνωσης	i ádhya kataskínosis
camping guide	ο κατάλογος κατασκήνωσης	o katáloghos kataskínosis
camping	το κάμπινγκ	to kámping
camping shop	το μαγαζί του κάμπινγκ	to maghazí too kámping
cancel	ακυρώνω	akiróno
candle	το κερί	to kerí
canoe	το κανό	to kanó
canoe (verb)	κάνω κανό	káno kanó
car trouble	η βλάβη	i vlávi
car	το αυτοκίνητο	to aftokínito
car papers	τα χαρτιά του αυτοκινήτου	ta chartyá too aftokinítoo
car park/parking space	το πάρκιγκ	to párking
car-deck	το κατάστρωμα για τα αυτοκίνητα	to katástroma ya ta aftokínita
carafe	η καράφα	i karáfa
caravan	το τροχόσπιτο	to trochóspito
cardigan	η ζακέτα	i zakéta
careful	προσεχτικός	prosechtikós
carriage (of train)	το βαγόνι	to vaghóni
carrot	το καρότο	to karóto
carton	η κούτα	i kóota
cash desk	το ταμείο	to tamío
casino	το καζίνο	to kazíno
cassette/cartridge	η κασέτα	i kaséta
castle	το κάστρο	o kástro
cat	η γάτα	i gháta

catalogue	ο κατάλογος	o katáloghos
cathedral	η μητρόπολη	i mitrópoli
cauliflower	το κουνουπίδι	to koonoopídhi
cave	η σπηλιά	i spilyá
celebrate	γιορτάζω	yortázo
celebration	η γιορτή	i yortí
cemetery	το νεκροταφείο	to nekrotafío
centimetre	ο πόντος	o póndos
centre	το κέντρο	to kéndro
chain	η αλυσίδα	i alisídha
chair	η καρέκλα	i karékla
chalet area	ο χώρος με μπάγκαλοου	o chóros me bángaló-óo
chambermaid	η καμαριέρα	i kamaryéra
champagne	η σαμπάνια	i sampánya
change (verb)	αλλάζω	aláozo
change the oil	αλλάζω τα λάδια	aláozo ta ládhya
change (small)	τα ψιλά	ta psilá
change (baby's nappy)	καθαρίζω	katharízo
chapel	το εξωκλήσι	to exoklísi
charter flight	η πτήση τσάρτερ	i ptísi-tsárter
chat up someone	ψωνίζω κάποιον	psonízo kápyon
cheap	φτηνός	ftinós
check (verb)	ελέγχω	eléncho
check in	τσεκάρω	tsekáro
cheers	στην υγειά σας	stiniyásas
cheese	το τυρί	to tirí
chemist's	το φαρμακείο	to farmakío
cheque	η επιταγή	i epitayí
cherries	τα κεράσια	ta kerásya
chess	το σκάκι	to skáki
chewing gum	η τσίχλα/η μαστίχα	i tsíchla/i mastícha
chicken	το κοτόπουλο	to kotópoolo
chicory	τα ραδίκια	ta radhíya
child seat (in car)	το παιδικό κάθισμα	to pedhikó káthizma
child	το παιδί	to pedhí
child seat (on bicycle)	η παιδική σέλα	i pedhikí séla
chin	το πηγούνι	to pighóoni
chips	πατάτες τηγανιτές	patátes tighanités
chocolate	η σοκολάτα	i sokoláta
choose	διαλέγω	dhialégho
christian name	το (μικρό) όνομα	to (mikró) ónoma
church	η εκκλησία	i eklisía
church service	η θεία λειτουργία	i thía litooryía
cigar	το πούρο	to póoro
cigarette paper	το τσιγαρόχαρτο	to tsigharócharto
cigarette	το τσιγάρο	to tsigháro
ciné-camera	η κινηματογραφική μηχανή	i kinimatoghrafikí michaní
circle	ο κύκλος	o kíklos
circus	το τσίρκο	to tsírko
city	η πόλη	i póli
classical concert	η κλασσική συναυλία	i klasikí sinavlía
clean (verb)	καθαρίζω	katharízo
clean	καθαρός	katharós
clear (adj.)	σαφής	safís
clearance sale	το ξεπούλημα	to xepóolima

closed off	κλειστός	*klistós*
closed	κλειστός	*klistós*
clothes peg	το μανταλάκι	*to mandaláki*
clothes	τα ρούχα	*ta róocha*
clothes hanger	η κρεμάστρα	*i kremástra*
coach	το πούλμαν	*to póolman*
coat	το παλτό	*to paltó*
cobbler	ο τσαγκάρης	*o tsangáris*
cockroach	η κατσαρίδα	*i katsarídha*
cod (dried)	ο μπακαλιάρος	*o bakalyáros*
coffee	ο καφές	*o kafés*
cold (disease)	το κρυολόγημα	*to kriolóyima*
cold	κρύος	*kríos*
cold meats	τα αλλαντικά	*ta alandiká*
collarbone	το κλειδοκόκαλο	*to klidhokókalo*
colleague	ο συνάδερφος	*o sinádherfos*
collision	η σύγκρουση	*i síngroosi*
cologne	η κολόνια	*i kolónya*
colour television	η έγχρωμη τηλεόραση	*i éngchromi tileórasi*
colour	το χρώμα	*to chróma*
coloured pencils	τα κραγιόνια	*ta krayónya*
comb	το χτένι	*to chténi*
come	έρχομαι	*érchome*
come back	ξαναέρχομαι	*xanaérchome*
compact disc	το κόμπακτ-ντισκ	*to kómpakt-disk*
compartment	το κουπέ	*to koopé*
complaint	το παράπονο	*to parápono*
complaints book	το βιβλίο παραπόνων	*to vivlío parapónon*
completely	τελείως	*telíos*
compliment	το κομπλιμέντο	*to kompliméndo*
compulsory	υποχρεωτικός	*ipochreotikós*
concert hall	η αίθουσα συναυλιών	*i éthoosa sinavlyón*
concert	η συναυλία	*i sinavlía*
concussion	η διάσειση εγκεφάλου	*i dhiásisi engkefáloo*
condom	το προφυλακτικό	*to profilaktikó*
confectioner	ο ζαχαροπλάστης	*o zacharoplástis*
congratulate	συγχαίρω	*sinchéro*
connection	η ανταπόκριση	*i andapókrisi*
constipation	η δυσκοιλιότητα	*i dhiskilyótita*
consulate	το προξενείο	*to proxenío*
consultation	η επίσκεψη	*i epískepsi*
contact lens	ο φακός επαφής	*o fakós epafís*
contact lens solution	το υγρό για φακούς επαφής	*to ighró ya fakóos epafís*
contagious	κολλητικός	*kolitikós*
contraceptive pill	το αντισυλληπτικό χάπι	*to andisiliptikó chápi*
contraceptive	το αντισυλληπτικό	*to andisiliptikó*
cook	ο μάγειρας	*o máyiras*
cook (verb)	μαγειρεύω	*mayirévo*
copper/bronze	χάλκινος	*chálkinos*
copy	το αντίγραφο	*to andíghrafo*
corkscrew	το τιρμπουσόν	*to tirbooshón*
corner	η γωνιά	*i ghonyá*
cornflower	το κορν φλάουερ	*to kornfláwer*
correct	σωστός	*sostós*
correspond	αλληλογραφώ	*aliloghrafó*
corridor	ο διάδρομος	*o dhiádhromos*

15

cot	το παιδικό κρεβάτι	to pedhikó kreváti
cotton wool	το βαμβάκι	o vamváki
cotton	το βαμβάκι	to vamváki
cough syrup	το σιρόπι για το βήχα	to sirópi ya to vícha
cough	ο βήχας	o víchas
counter	η θυρίδα	i thirídha
country	η χώρα	i chóra
country (dialling) code	ο αριθμός της χώρας	o arithmós tis chóras
countryside	η εξοχή	i exohí
courgette	το κολοκυθάκι	to kolokitháki
course of treatment	η θεραπεία	i therapía
cousin (female)	η ξαδέρφη	i xadhérfi
cousin (male)	ο ξάδερφος	o xádherfos
crab	ο κάβουρας	o kávooras
cream (ointment)	η κρέμα	i kréma
cream	το ανθόγαλα	to anthóghala
credit card	η πιστωτική κάρτα	i pistotikí kárta
crisps	τα τσιπς	ta tsips
cross the road	περνώ το δρόμο	perno to dhrómo
crossing	το πέρασμα	to pérazma
cry (verb)	κλαίω	kléo
cubic metre	το κυβικό μέτρο	to kivikó métro
cucumber	το αγγούρι	to anghóori
cuff links	τα μανικετόκουμπα	ta maniketókoomba
cup	το φλιτζάνι	to flidzáni
curly	σγουρός	zghoorós
current (water)	το ρεύμα	to révma
current (electricity)	το ρεύμα	to révma
cushion	το μαξιλαράκι	to maxilaráki
custard	η κρέμα	i kréma
customary	συνηθισμένος	sinithizménos
customs officer	ο τελώνης	o telónis
customs check	ο τελωνιακός έλεγχος	o teloniakós élenchos
customs	το τελωνείο	to telonío
cut (verb)	κόβω	kóvo
cutlery	τα μαχαιροπήρουνα	ta maheropíroona
cyclist	ο ποδηλάτης	o podhilátis

D

damage	η βλάβη	i vlávi
dance (verb)	χορεύω	chorévo
dandruff	η πιτυρίδα	i pitirídha
danger	ο κίνδυνος	o kíndhinos
dangerous	επικίνδυνος	epikíndhinos
dark	σκοτεινός	skotinós
daughter	η κόρη	i kóri
day after tomorrow	μεθαύριο	methávrio
day	η μέρα	i méra
day (24 hours)	το μερόνυχτο	to merónichto
day before yesterday	προχτές	prochtés
dead	νεκρός	nekrós
decaffeinated	χωρίς καφείνη	chorís kafeíni
December	ο Δεκέμβριος	o dekémvrios
deck chair	η ξαπλώστρα, η σαιζ-λόνγκ	i xaplóstra, i sezlóng
declare (customs)	δηλώνω	dhilóno
deep	βαθύς	vathís

deep-frozen	καταψυγμένος	katapsighménos
deep-sea diving	η κατάδυση σε μεγάλο βάθος	i katádhisi se meghálo váthos
defective	ελαττωματικός	elatomatikós
degrees	οι βαθμοί	i vathmí
delay (noun)	η καθυστέρηση	i kathistérisi
delicious	εξαιρετικός	exeretikós
dentist	ο οδοντογιατρός	o odhondoyatrós
dentures	η μασέλα	maséla
deodorant	το αποσμητικό	to apozmitikó
department store	ο εμπορικός οίκος	o emborikós íkos
department	το τμήμα	to tmíma
departure time	η ώρα αναχώρησης	i óra anachórisis
departure	η αναχώρηση	i anachórisi
depilatory cream	το αποτριχωτικό	to apotrichotikó
deposit	η εγγύηση	i engíisi
dessert	το επιδόρπιο	to epidhórpyo
destination	ο προορισμός	o pro-orizmós
details (personal etc.)	τα στοιχεία	ta stihía
develop (film)	εμφανίζω	emfanízo
diabetic	ο διαβητικός	o dhiavitikós
dial	παίρνω	pérno
diamond	το διαμάντι	to dhiamándi
diarrhoea	η διάρροια	i dhiária
dictionary	το λεξικό	to lexikó
diesel oil	το (λάδι) ντήζελ	to (ládhi) dízel
diet	η δίαιτα	i dhíeta
difficulty	η δυσκολία	i dhiskolía
dine	δειπνώ	dhipnó
dining room	η τραπεζαρία	i trapezaría
dining-car	το βαγόνι-εστιατόριο	to vaghóni-estiatório
dinner jacket	το σμόκιν	to smókin
dinner	το δείπνο	to dhípno
direction	η κατεύθυνση	i katéfthinsi
directly	κατ' ευθείαν	katefthían
dirty	βρόμικος	vrómikos
disabled	ανάπηρος	anápiros
disco	η ντίσκο	i dísko
discount	η έκπτωση	i ékptosi
dish of the day	το πιάτο της ημέρας	to pyáto tis iméras
disinfectant	το απολυμαντικό	to apolimandikó
displeased, I am	μου κακοφαίνεται	moo kakofenete
distance	η απόσταση	i apóstasi
distilled water	το διυλισμένο νερό	to dhiilizméno neró
disturb	ενοχλώ	enochló
disturbance	η διατάραξη	i dhiatáraxi
dive	βουτώ	vootó
diving	η κατάδυση	i katádhisi
diving gear	τα εξαρτήματα κατάδυσης	ta exartímata katádhisis
diving board	ο βατήρας	o vatíras
divorced	χωρισμένος	chorizménos
dizzy	ζαλισμένος	zalizménos
do night duty	διανυκτερεύω	dhianikterévo
do	κάνω	káno
doctor	ο γιατρός	o yatrós
dog	ο σκύλος	o skílos

doll	η κούκλα	o kóokla
domestic (e.g. flights)	εσωτερικός	esoterikós
door	η πόρτα	i pórta
double/for two	για δύο άτομα	ya dhío átoma
down	κάτω	káto
drachma	η δραχμή	i dhrachmí
draught, there's a	κάνει ρεύμα	káni révma
dream	ονειρεύομαι	onirévome
dress	το φόρεμα	to fórema
dressing gown	η ρόμπα	i róba
dried fruit	ξηροί καρποί	xirí karpí
drink (verb)	πίνω	píno
drink	το ποτό	to potó
drinking chocolate	το γάλα με κακάο	to ghála me kakáo
drinking water	το πόσιμο νερό	to pósimo neró
drive	οδηγώ	odhighó
driver	ο οδηγός	o odhighós
driving licence	η άδεια οδηγήσεως	i ádhya odhiyíseos
drought	η ξηρασία	i xirasía
dry clean	στεγνοκαθαρίζω	steghnokatharízo
dry cleaner's	το στεγνοκαθαριστήριο	to steghnokatharistírio
dry (verb)	στεγνώνω	steghnóno
dry	ξηρός	xirós
dry shampoo	το στεγνό σαμπουάν	to steghnó sampwán
dummy	η πιπίλα	i pipíla
during the day	την ημέρα	tin iméra
during	κατά την διάρκεια	katá ti dhiarkía

E

ear, node and throat specialist	ο ωτορινολαρυγγο-λόγος	o otorinolaringhológhos
ear drops	οι σταγόνες για τα αυτιά	i staghónes ya ta aftyá
ear	το αυτί	to avtí
early	νωρίς	norís
earrings	τα σκουλαρίκια	ta skoolaríkya
earth	το χώμα	to chóma
earthenware	η κεραμική	i keramikí
east	η ανατολή	i anatolí
easy	εύκολος	éfkolos
eat	τρώω	tró-o
eczema	το έκζεμα	to ékzema
eel	το χέλι	to héli
egg	το αυγό	to avghó
elastic band	το λαστιχάκι	to lasticháki
electric	ηλεκτρικός	ilektrikós
electrical connection	η ηλεκτρική σύνδεση	i ilektrikí síndhesi
embassy	η πρεσβεία	i prezvía
emergency signal	το σήμα κινδύνου	to síma kindhínoo
emergency triangle	το τρίγωνο κινδύνου	to tríghono kindhínoo
emergency exit	η έξοδος κινδύνου	i éxodhos kindhínoo
emergency number	ο αριθμός του συναγερμού	o arithmós too sinayermóo
empty	άδειος	ádhyos
engaged (phone)	κατειλημμένο	katiliméno
England	η Αγγλία	i anglía
English	τα αγγλικά	ta angliká

Englishman/woman	ο Αγγλος/η Αγγλίδα	o ánglos/i anglídha
enjoy	απολαμβάνω	apolamváno
entertainment	η διασκέδαση	i dhiaskédhasi
entertainment guide (Athens only)	το Αθηνόραμα	to athinórama
entrance	η είσοδος	i ísodhos
envelope	ο φάκελος	o fákelos
environment	το περιβάλλον	to periválon
escort	η/ο συνοδός	i/o sinodhós
essentially	ουσιαστικά	oosiastiká
evening dress	η βραδινή ενδυμασία	i vradhiní endhimasía
evening	το βράδυ	to vrádhi
evening meal	το δείπνο	to dhípno
event	το γεγονός	to yeghonós
every time	κάθε φορά	káthe forá
everything	τα πάντα	ta pánda
everywhere	παντού	pandóo
examine	εξετάζω	exetázo
excavations	οι ανασκαφές	i anaskafés
excellent	υπέροχος	ipérochos
exchange (money)	αλλάζω	alázo
exchange	ανταλλάσσω	antaláso
excursion	η εκδρομή	i ekdhromí
exhibition	η έκθεση	i ékthesi
exit	η έξοδος	i éxodhos
expenses	τα έξοδα	ta éxodha
expensive	ακριβός	akrivós
explain	εξηγώ	exighó
express train	η ταχεία	i tahía
external	εξωτερικός	exoterikós
eye specialist	ο οφθαλμίατρος	o ofthalmíatros
eye	το μάτι	to máti
eyedrops	οι σταγόνες για τα μάτια	i staghónes ya ta mátya
eyeliner	το μολύβι για τα μάτια	to molívi ya ta mátya

F

face	το πρόσωπο	to prósopo
factory	το εργοστάσιο	to erghostásyo
fall	πέφτω	péfto
family	η οικογένεια	i ikoyénya
famous	ξακουστός	xakoostós
far away	μακριά	makriá
farm	το αγρόκτημα	to aghróktima
farmer	ο γεωργός	o yeorghós
fashion	η μόδα	i módha
father	ο πατέρας	o patéras
fax (verb)	στέλνω ένα φαξ	stélno éna fax
February	ο Φεβρουάριος	o fevrooários
feel like	έχω διάθεση	écho dhiáthesi
feel like	αισθάνομαι	esthánome
ferry	το φέρρυ-μπωτ	to féribot
festival	η γιορτή	i yortí
fever	ο πυρετός	o piretós
fill (tooth)	σφραγίζω	sfrayízo

Word list

15

fill/top up	γεμίζω	yemízo
fill out	συμπληρώνω	simpliróno
filling	το σφράγισμα	to sfráyizma
film	η ταινία	i tenía
film (camera)	το φιλμ	to film
filter	το φίλτρο	to fíltro
find	βρίσκω	vrísko
fine	η κλήση	i klísi
finger	το δάχτυλο	to dháchtilo
fingernail	το νύχι	to níhi
fire escape	η σκάλα πυρκαγιάς	i skála pirkayás
fire	η φωτιά	i fotyá
fire (accidental)	η πυρκαγιά	i pirkayá
fire extinguisher	ο πυροσβεστήρας	o pirosvestíras
fire brigade	η πυροσβεστική υπηρεσία	i pirosvestikí ipiresía
first aid	οι πρώτες βοήθειες	i prótes voíthyes
first class	η πρώτη θέση	i próti thési
first	πρώτος	prótos
fish (verb)	ψαρεύω	psarévo
fish	το ψάρι	to psári
fishing rod	το αγκίστρι	to angístri
fitness centre	το γυμναστήριο	to yimnastírio
fitting room	το δοκιμαστήριο	to dhokimastíryo
fix	φτιάχνω	ftyáchno
flag	η σημαία	i siméa
flash bulb	η λάμπα φλας	i lámpa flash
flash gun	το φλας	to flash
flash cubes	οι λάμπες φλας	i lámpes flash
flea market	το παλιατζίδικο	to paliatzídhiko
flight	η πτήση	i ptísi
flight number	ο αριθμός της πτήσης	o arithmós tis ptísis
flood	η πλημμύρα	i plimíra
floor	ο όροφος	o órofos
flour	το αλεύρι	to alévri
flu	η γρίπη	i ghrípi
fly	η μύγα	i mígha
fly (verb)	πετώ	petó
flyover	η οδογέφυρα	i odhoyéfira
foggy, it is	έχει ομίχλη	éhi omíchli
folding caravan	το λυόμενο τροχόσπιτο	to liómeno trochóspito
folkloristic	λαογραφικός	laoghrafikós
follow	ακολουθώ	akoloothó
food poisoning	η τροφική δηλητηρίαση	i trofikí dhilitiríasi
food	το φαγητό	to fayitó
food	τα τρόφιμα	ta trófima
foot	το πόδι	to pódhi
football	το ποδόσφαιρο	to podhósfero
football match	ο ποδοσφαιρικός αγώνας	o podhosferikós aghónas
for hire	ενοικιάζεται	enikyázete
forbidden, it is	απαγορεύεται	apaghorévete
forehead	το μέτωπο	to métopo
foreign	εξωτερικός	exoterikós
forget	ξεχνάω	xechnáo
fork	το πηρούνι	to pirόoni
form	το έντυπο	to éndipo

Word list

15

fort	το κάστρο	to kástro
fountain	το συντριβάνι	to sindriváni
frame	ο σκελετός	o skeletós
free	ελεύθερος	eléftheros
free time	η ελεύθερη ώρα	i eléftheri óra
freeze	παγώνω	paghóno
French	τα γαλλικά	ta ghaliká
French bread	το ψωμί μπαστούνι	to psomí bastóoni
fresh	φρέσκος	fréskos
Friday	η Παρασκευή	i paraskeví
fried	τηγανητός	tighanitós
fried egg	το αυγό μάτι	to avghó máti
friend	ο φίλος	o fílos
friendly	ευγενικός	evyenikós
fringe	η φράντζα	i frándza
fritter	η τηγανίτα	i tighaníta
front, at the	μπροστά	brostá
frozen	καταψυγμένος	katapsighménos
fruit	το φρούτο	to fróoto
fruit juice	ο χυμός	o chimós
frying pan	το τηγάνι	to tigháni
full	γεμάτος	yemátos

G

gallery (theatre)	ο εξώστης	o exóstis
game	το παιχνίδι	to pechnídhi
garage	το γκαράζ	to garáz
garbage bag	η σακούλα σκουπιδιών	i sakóola skoopidhyón
garden	ο κήπος	o kípos
gauze	η γάζα	i gháza
gear	η ταχύτητα	i tahítita
gel	το τζελ	to dzel
gentleman	ο κύριος	o kírios
German	τα γερμανικά	ta yermaniká
get off/out	κατεβαίνω	katevéno
get lost	χάνω το δρόμο	cháno to dhrómo
gift	το δώρο	to dhóro
girl	το κορίτσι	to korítsi
girl friend	η φίλη	i fíli
giro cheque	η ταχυδρομική επιταγή	i tahidhromikí epitayí
giro card	η ταχυδρομική κάρτα	i tahidhromikí kárta
glass	το ποτήρι	to potíri
glasses (sun-, reading-)	τα γυαλιά	ta yalyá
gliding	η ανεμοπορία	i anemoporía
glove	το γάντι	to ghándi
glue	η κόλλα	i kóla
go out	βγαίνω έξω	vyéno éxo
go back	γυρίζω	yirízo
go	πηγαίνω	piyéno
goat's cheese	το κατσικίσιο τυρί	to katsikísyo tirí
gold	το χρυσάφι	to chrisáfi
gold-plated	επίχρυσος	epíchrisos
golf course	το γήπεδο του γκολφ	to yípedho too golf
golf	το γκολφ	to golf
good afternoon	καλημέρα	kaliméra
good night	καληνύχτα	kaliníchta
good day	καλημέρα	kaliméra

good luck	η ευτυχία	*i eftihía*
good morning	καλημέρα	*kaliméra*
good evening	καλησπέρα	*kalispéra*
goodbye	γειά σας, γειά σου	*yásas, yásoo*
goodbye (farewell)	ο αποχαιρετισμός	*o apoheretizmós*
gram	το γραμμάριο	*to ghramário*
grandchild	το εγγόνι	*to engóni*
grandfather	ο παππούς	*o papóos*
grandmother	η γιαγιά	*i yayá*
grape juice	ο χυμός σταφυλιών	*o chimós stafilyón*
grapefruit	η φράπα	*i frápa*
grapes	τα σταφύλια	*ta stafílya*
gratis	δωρεάν	*dhoreán*
grave	ο τάφος	*o táfos*
grease	τα λίπη	*ta lípi*
green card	η πράσινη κάρτα	*i prásini kárta*
green	πράσινος	*prásinos*
greet	χαιρετίζω	*heretízo*
greetings	τα χαιρετίσματα	*ta heretízmata*
grey	γκρίζος	*grízos*
grill (verb)	ψήνω στα κάρβουνα	*psíno sta kárvoona*
grilled	ψητός	*psitós*
grocer	ο μπακάλης	*o bakális*
ground	το χώμα	*to chóma*
group	το γκρουπ	*to groop*
guest house	η πανσιόν	*i pansyón*
guide (person)	ο ξεναγός	*o xenaghós*
guidebook	ο οδηγός	*o odhighós*
guided tour	η ξενάγηση	*i xenáyisi*
guilt	η ενοχή	*i enohí*
gynaecologist	ο γυναικολόγος	*o yinekológhos*

H

hair cream	το βερνίκι για τα μαλλιά	*to verníki ya ta malyá*
hair	τα μαλλιά	*ta malyá*
hairdresser	ο κομμωτής	*o komotís*
hairpins	οι καρφίτσες	*i karfítses*
half kilo	το μισό κιλό	*to misó kiló*
half	μισό	*misó*
half-full	μισογεμάτος	*misoyemátos*
ham	το ζαμπόν	*to zambón*
hammer	το σφυρί	*to sfirí*
hand brake	το χειρόφρενο	*to hirófreno*
hand	το χέρι	*to héri*
handbag	η τσάντα	*i tsánda*
handmade	χειροποίητος	*hiropíitos*
handicraft	η χειροτεχνία	*i hirotechnía*
handkerchief	το μαντήλι	*to mandíli*
handsome	ωραίος	*oréos*
happy	χαρούμενος	*charóomenos*
harbour	το λιμάνι	*to limáni*
hard	σκληρός	*sklirós*
hat	το καπέλο	*to kapélo*
hayfever	ο αλλεργικός κατάρρους	*o aleryikós katároos*
hazelnut	το φουντούκι	*to foondóoki*

head	το κεφάλι	to kefáli
headache	ο πονοκέφαλος	o ponokéfalos
health	η υγεία	i iyía
heart patient	ο καρδιακός	o kardhiakós
heart	η καρδιά	i kardhyá
heater	το καλοριφέρ	to kalorifér
heavy	βαρύς	varís
hedge	ο φράχτης	o fráchtis
heel (of shoe)	το τακούνι	to takóoni
hello	γειά σας, γειά σου	yásas, yásoo
helmet	το κράνος	to krános
help	η βοήθεια	i voíthya
help (verb)	βοηθώ	voithó
herb tea	το τσάι του βουνού	to tsái too voonóo
herbs	τα μπαχαρικά	ta bachariká
here	εδώ	edhó
herring (smoked)	η ρέγγα	i rénga
high tide	η παλίρροια	i palíria
high chair	η παιδική καρέκλα	i pedhikí karékla
high	ψηλός	psilós
hiking	η πεζοπορία	i pezoporía
hip	ο γοφός	o ghofós
hire	νοικιάζω	nikyázo
hitch-hiking	το ωτοστόπ	to otostóp
hobby	το χόμπυ	to chóbi
hold-up	η επίθεση	i epíthesi
holiday cottage	το εξοχικό σπιτάκι	to exohikó spitáki
holiday (public)	η γιορτή	i yortí
holidays	οι διακοπές	i dhiakopés
homesickness	η νοσταλγία	i nostalyía
honest	τίμιος	tímyos
honey	το μέλι	to méli
horizontal	οριζόντιος	orizóndios
horrible	απαίσιος	apésios
horse	το άλογο	to álogho
hospital	το νοσοκομείο	to nosokomío
hospitality	η φιλοξενία	i filoxenía
hot	ζεστός	zestós
hot (spicy)	πικάντικος	pikándikos
hot spring	η θερμική πηγή	i thermikí piyí
hot-water bottle	η θερμοφόρα	i thermofóra
hotel	το ξενοδοχείο	to xenodhohío
hour	η ώρα	i óra
house	το σπίτι	to spíti
household items	τα οικιακά αντικείμενα	ta ikyaká andikímena
housewife	η νοικοκυρά	i nikokirá
how	πώς;	pos?
how far?	πόσο μακριά;	póso makriá?
how much?	πόσο;	póso?
how long?	πόσο καιρό;	póso kyeró?
hundred grams	εκατό γραμμάρια	ekató ghramárya
hunger	η πείνα	i pína
hurricane	ο τυφώνας	o tifónas
hurry (be in a)	βιάζομαι	vyázome
husband	ο σύζυγος	o sízighos
hut	η καλύβα	i kalíva
hyperventilation	η υπεροξυγόνωση	i iperoxighónosi

I

ice	ο πάγος	o pághos
ice-cream	το παγωτό	to paghotó
ice-cubes	τα παγάκια	ta paghákya
idea	η ιδέα	i idhéa
identification	η ταυτότητα	i taftótita
identify	αναγνωρίζω	anaghnorízo
ignition key	το κλειδί επαφής	to klidhí epafís
illness	η αρρώστια	i aróstia
illustrated book	το εικονογραφημένο βιβλίο	to ikonoghrafiméno vivlío
imagine	φαντάζομαι	fandázome
immediately	αμέσως	amésos
import duty	τα εισαγωγικά τέλη	ta isaghoyiká téli
impossible	αδύνατος	adhínatos
in front of	μπροστά σε	brostá se
in	σε	se
in front	μπροστά	brostá
in safe-keeping	σε φύλαξη	se fílaxi
in the evening/at night	το βράδυ	to vrádhi
included (it is)	συμπεριλαμβάνεται	simperilamvánete
indicate	δείχνω	dhíchno
indicator	το φλας	to flash
indigestion	η δυσπεψία	i dhispepsía
inflammation	η φλεγμονή	i fleghmoní
information office	το γραφείο πληροφοριών	to ghrafío pliroforyón
information	οι πληροφορίες	i plirofóries
information (piece of)	η πληροφορία	i pliroforía
injection	η ένεση	i énesi
injured	λαβωμένος	lavoménos
inner tube	το εσωτερικό λάστιχο	to esoterikó lásticho
innocent	αθώος	athóos
insect	το έντομο	to éndomo
insect repellent	λάδι για τα κουνούπια	ládhi ya ta koonóopya
insect bite	το τσίμπημα εντόμου	to tsímbima endómoo
inside	μέσα	mésa
insole	η εσωτερική σόλα	i esoterikí sóla
instructions for use	οι οδηγίες χρήσεως	i odhiyíes chríseos
insurance	η ασφάλεια	i asfálya
internal	εσωτερικός	esoterikós
international	διεθνής	dhiethnís
interpreter	ο διερμηνέας	o dhierminéas
intersection	η διασταύρωση	i dhiastávrosi
interval	το διάλειμμα	to dhiálima
introduce	γνωρίζω	ghnorízo
introduce myself	συστήνομαι	sistínome
invite	προσακλώ	proskaló
iodine	το ιώδιο	to iódhio
Ireland	η Ιρλανδία	i irlandhía
Irishman	ο Ιρλανδός/η Ιρλανδέζα	o irlandhós/i irlandhéza
iron	το σίδερο	to sídhero
iron (verb)	σιδερώνω	sidheróno
ironing board	η σανίδα σιδερώματος	i sanídha sidherómatos
island	το νησί	to nisí
Italian	τα ιταλικά	ta italiká

Word list

15

itch	η φαγούρα	i faghóora
item of clothing	το ρούχο	to róocho
itinerary	το δρομολόγιο	to dhromolóyo

J

jack	ο γρύλλος	o ghrílos
jacket	η ζακέτα	i zakéta
jam	η μαρμελάδα	i marmeládha
January	ο Ιανουάριος	o yanooários
jaw	το σαγόνι	to saghóni
jellyfish	η μέδουσα	i médhoosa
jeweller	ο χρυσοχόος	o chrisochóos
jewellery	τα κοσμήματα	ta kozmímata
jog (running)	το τρέξιμο	to tréximo
joke	το αστείο	to astío
juice	ο χυμός	o himós
July	ο Ιούλιος	o yóolios
jump leads	το καλώδιο εκκίνησης	to kalódhio ekkínisis
jumper	το πουλόβερ	o poolóver
June	ο Ιούνιος	o yóonios
junk shop	το παλιατζίδικο	to paliadzídhiko

K

kettle	ο βραστήρας	o vrastíras
key	το κλειδί	to klidhí
kilo	το κιλό	to kiló
kilometer	το χιλιόμετρο	to hilyómetro
king	ο βασιλιάς	o vasilyás
kiosk	το περίπτερο	to períptero
kiss	το φιλί	to filí
kiss (verb)	φιλώ	filó
kitchen	η κουζίνα	i koozína
knee	το γόνατο	to ghónato
knife	το μαχαίρι	to machéri
knit	πλέκω	pléko
know (person)	γνωρίζω	ghnorízo
know	ξέρω	xéro

L

lace	η δαντέλα	i dhantéla
ladies' toilet	η τουαλέτα γυναικών	i twaléta yinekón
lady	η κυρία	i kiría
lake	η λίμνη	i límni
lamb chop	το παϊδάκι	to paidháki
lamp	η λάμπα	i lámpa
land (verb)	προσγειώνομαι	prosyiónome
lane (on road)	η λωρίδα	i lorídha
language	η γλώσσα	i ghlóssa
lard	το λαρδί	to lardhí
large	μεγάλος	meghálos
last	τελευταίος	teleftéos
last night	χθες τη νύχτα	chthes ti níchta
late	αργά	arghá
latest, at the	το αργότερο	to arghótero
laugh	γελάω	yeláo
launderette	το πλυντήριο	to plindírio
lavatory	η τουαλέτα	i twaléta

law (studies)	τα νομικά	ta nomiká
lawyer	ο δικηγόρος	o dhikighóros
laxative	το καθαρτικό	to kathartikó
leaking	τρυπημένος	tripiménos
leather	το δέρμα	to dhérma
leather goods	τα δερμάτινα είδη	ta dhermátina ídhi
leave (verb)	φεύγω	févgho
leek	το πράσο	to práso
left luggage locker	η θυρίδα αποσκευών	i thirídha aposkevón
left (adj.)	αριστερός	aristerós
left (on/to the)	αριστερά	aristerá
left luggage office	ο χώρος αποσκευών	o chóros aposkevón
leg	το πόδι	to pódhi
lemon	το λεμόνι	to lemóni
lemonade	η λεμονάδα	i lemonádha
lens	ο φακός	o fakós
lentils	οι φακές	i fakés
less	λιγότερο	lighótero
lesson	το μάθημα	to máthima
letter	το γράμμα	to ghrámma
lettuce	το μαρούλι	to maróoli
level crossing	η διάβαση	i dhiávasi
library	η βιβλιοθήκη	i vivliothíki
lie down	ξαπλώνομαι	xaplónome
lie	λέω ψέματα	léo psémata
lifeguard	ο ακτοφύλακας	o aktofílakas
lift	το ασανσέρ/ ο ανελκυστήρας	to asansér/o anelkistíras
light (colour)	ανοιχτός	anichtós
light (weight)	ελαφρός	elafrós
light	το φως	to fos
lighter	ο αναπτήρας	o anaptíras
lighthouse	ο φάρος	o fáros
lightning	ο κεραυνός	o keravnós
like, I	μ' αρέσει	marési
line	η γραμμή	i ghramí
linen	το λινό	to linó
lipstick	το κραγιόν	to krayón
listen	ακούω	akóo-o
literature	η λογοτεχνία	i loghotechnía
litre	το λίτρο	to lítro
little	λίγος	líghos
live	μένω	méno
live together	συγκατοικώ	singkatikó
lively	ζωηρός	zoirós
lobster	ο αστακός	o astakós
local	τοπικός	topikós
local (dialling) code	ο κωδικός της πόλης	o kodhikós tis pólis
lock	η κλειδαριά	i klidharyá
long (tall)	μακρύς	makrís
long (of time)	πολύς	polís
look	κοιτάζω	kitázo
lorry	το καμιόνι	to kamyóni
lose	χάνω	cháno
loss	ο χαμός, η απώλεια	o chamós, i apólya
lost property	τα ευρεθέντα αντικείμενα	ta evrethénda andikímena

lost	χαμένος	*chaménos*
lotion	η λοσιόν	*i losión*
loud	δυνατά	*dhinatá*
love with, be in	είμαι ερωτευμένος με	*íme erotevménos me*
love (verb)	αγαπώ	*aghapó*
love	η αγάπη	*i agápi*
low tide	η άμπωτη	*i ámboti*
low	χαμηλός	*chamilós*
luggage	οι αποσκευές	*i aposkevés*
luggage locker	η θυρίδα αποσκευών	*i thirídha aposkevón*
lunch	το γεύμα	*to yévma*
lungs	οι πνεύμονες	*i pnévmones*

M

machine	η μηχανή	*i michaní*
magazine	το περιοδικό	*to periodhikó*
mail	το ταχυδρομείο	*to tahidhromío*
main road	ο μεγάλος δρόμος	*o meghálos dhrómos*
main post-office	το κεντρικό ταχυδρομείο	*to kendrikó tahidhromío*
make an appointment/ a date	δίνω ραντεβού	*dhíno randevóo*
make love	κάνω έρωτα	*káno érota*
man	ο άντρας	*o ándras*
manager	ο διαχειριστής	*o dhiahiristís*
mandarin (orange)	το μανταρίνι	*to mandaríni*
manicure	το μανικιούρ	*to manikýoor*
map	ο χάρτης	*o chártis*
marble	το μάρμαρο	*to mármaro*
March	ο Μάρτιος	*o mártios*
margarine	η μαργαρίνη	*i margharíni*
marina	η μαρίνα	*i marína*
market	η αγορά	*i aghorá*
marriage	ο γάμος	*o ghámos*
married	παντρεμένος	*pandreménos*
married, get	παντρεύομαι	*pandrévome*
massage	το μασάζ	*to masáz*
matt (photographs)	ματ	*mat*
match	ο αγώνας	*o aghónas*
matches	τα σπίρτα	*ta spírta*
May	Ο Μάιος	*o máios*
maybe	ίσως	*ísos*
mayonnaise	η μαγιονέζα	*i mayionéza*
mayor	ο δήμαρχος	*o dhímarchos*
meal	το γεύμα	*to yévma*
mean	σημαίνω	*siméno*
means	το μέσο	*to méso*
meat	το κρέας	*to kréas*
medication	το φάρμακο	*to fármako*
medicine (liquid)	το σιρόπι	*to sirópi*
medicine	το φάρμακο	*to fármako*
melon	το πεπόνι	*to pepóni*
membership	η ιδιότητα του μέλους	*i idhiótita too méloos*
menstruate	έχω περίοδο	*écho período*
menstruation	η περίοδος	*i períodhos*
menu of the day	το μενού της ημέρας	*to menóo tis iméras*
menu	το μενού, ο κατάλογος	*to menóo o katáloghos*

Word list

15

message	η παραγγελία	i parangelía
metal	το μέταλλο	to métalo
meter	ο μετρητής	o metritís
metre	το μέτρο	to métro
middle, in the	στη μέση	sti mési
migraine	η ημικρανία	i imikranía
mild (tobacco)	ελαφρός	elafrós
milk	το γάλα	to ghála
milk products	τα προϊόντα γάλακτος	ta proiónda ghálaktos
milk for coffee	το γάλα για τον καφέ	to ghála ya tongafé
millimetre	το χιλιοστόμετρο	to hilyostómetro
milometer	το κοντέρ	to kontér
mince	ο κιμάς	o kimás
mineral water	το μεταλλικό νερό	to metalikó neró
minute	το λεπτό	to leptó
mirror	ο καθρέφτης	o kathréftis
miss (I)	μου λείπει	moo lípi
missing (is)	λείπει	lípi
missing (person)	χαμένος	chaménos
mist	η ομίχλη	i omíchli
mistake	το λάθος	to láthos
mistaken, be	κάνω λάθος	káno láthos
Mister	ο κύριος	o kírios
misunderstanding	η παρεξήγηση	i parexíyisi
mocha	η μόκα	i móka
modern art	η σύγχρονη τέχνη	i síngchroni téchni
molar	ο τραπεζίτης	o trapezítis
moment	η στιγμή	i stighmí
monastery	το μοναστήρι	to monastíri
Monday	η Δευτέρα	i deftéra
money	τα λεφτά	ta leftá
month	ο μήνας	o mínas
moped	το μηχανάκι	to michanáki
morning (in the)	το πρωί	to proí
morning-after-pill	το μόρνινγκ-άφτερ-χάπι	to mórning-áfter-chápi
mosque	το τζαμί	to dzamí
mosquito	το κουνούπι	to koonóopi
motel	το μοτέλ	to motél
mother	η μητέρα	i mitéra
motorboat	η βενζινάκατος	i venzinákatos
motorcycle	η μοτοσικλέτα	i motosikléta
motorway	η εθνική οδός	i ethnikí odhós
mountain boots	τα παπούτσια ορειβασίας	ta papóotsya orivasías
mountain hut	το ορειβατικό καταφύγιο	to orivatikó katafíyo
mountain	το βουνό	to voonó
mountaineering	η ορειβασία	i orivasía
mouse	το ποντίκι	to pondíki
mouth	το στόμα	to stóma
move back	κάνω πίσω	káno píso
Mrs	η κυρία	i kiría
much/many	πολύς	polís
multistorey carpark	το σκεπασμένο πάρκινγκ	to skepazméno párking
muscle spasm	ο σπασμός	o spazmós
muscle	ο μυς	o mis

museum	το μουσείο	to moosío
mushrooms	τα μανιτάρια	ta manitárya
music	η μουσική	i moosikí
musical (show)	η μουσική κωμωδία	i moosikí komodhía
mussels	τα μύδια	ta mídhya
mustard	η μουστάρδα	i moostárdha
my name is	λέγομαι/με λένε	léghome/me léne

N

nail varnish remover	το ασετόν	to asetón
nail varnish	το βερνίκι νυχιών	to verníki nihyón
nail scissors	το ψαλιδάκι για τα νύχια	to psalidháki yia ta níhya
nail	το καρφί	to karfí
nail file	η λίμα για τα νύχια	i líma ya ta níhya
naked	γυμνός	yimnós
napkin	η πετσέτα	i petséta
nappy	η πάνα	i pána
National Health Office	το ταμείο ασθενείας	to tamío asthenías
nationality	η υπηκοότητα	i ipikoótita
naturally	φυσικά	fisiká
nature	η φύση	i físi
nauseous, I feel	ανακατεύεται το στομάχι μου	anakatévete to stomáchi moo
near	κοντά	kondá
near to	κοντά σε	kondá se
necessary	αναγκαίος	anangéos
neck	ο σβέρκος	o zvérkos
nectarine	το νεκταρίνι	to nektaríni
needle	το βελόνι	to velóni
negative	το αρνητικό	to arnitikó
neighbours	οι γείτονες	i yítones
nephew	ο ανιψιός	o anipsyós
never	ποτέ	poté
new	καινούριος	kenóorios
news	τα νέα	ta néa
newspaper	η εφημερίδα	i efimerídha
next	επόμενος	epómenos
next to	δίπλα σε	dhípla se
nice-looking	ωραίος	oréos
nice (people, things and events)	καλός	kalós
niece	η ανιψιά	i anipsyá
night life	η νυχτερινή ζωή	i nichteriní zoí
night	το βράδυ	to vrádhi
night	η νύχτα	i níchta
nightclub	το νυχτερινό κέντρο	to nichterinó kéndro
no	όχι	óhi
no overtaking	απαγορεύεται η προσπέραση	apaghorévete i prospérasi
no one	κανένας	kanénas
noise	ο θόρυβος	o thórivos
non-stop	χωρίς σταθμούς	chorís stathmóos
nonsense	οι σαχλαμάρες	i sachlamáres
normal	κανονικός	kanonikós
north	ο βοριάς	o voryás

nose	η μύτη	i míti
nose-drops	οι σταγόνες για τη μύτη	i staghónes ya ti míti
nosebleed	η ρινορραγία	i rinorayía
notepaper	το χαρτί αλληλογραφίας	to chartí aliloghrafías
nothing	τίποτα	típota
November	ο Νοέμβριος	o noémvrios
nowhere	πουθενά	poothená
nude	γυμνός	yimnós
nudism	ο γυμνισμός	o yimnizmós
nudist beach	η πλαζ για γυμνιστές	i plaz ya yimnistés
number plate	ο αριθμός κυκλοφορίας	o arithmós kikloforías
number	ο αριθμός	o arithmós
nurse	η νοσοκόμα	i nosokóma
nutmeg	το μοσχοκάρυδο	to moschokáridho

O

object	το αντικείμενο	to andikímeno
occupied/taken	κατειλημμένος	katiliménos
October	ο Οκτώβριος	o októvrios
off (of meat)	χαλασμένος	chalazménos
off-licence	η κάβα	i káva
offer	προσφέρω	prosféro
office	το γραφείο	to ghrafío
oil	το λάδι	to ládhi
oil level	η στάθμη του λαδιού	i státhmi too ladhyóo
ointment for burns	η αλοιφή για εγκαύματα	i alifí ya engkávmata
ointment	η αλοιφή	i alifí
OK	εντάξει	endáxi
old	μεγάλος	meghálos
olive oil	το ελαιόλαδο	to eleóladho
olives	οι ελιές	i elyés
omelette	η ομελέτα	i omeléta
on	πάνω σε	páno se
onboard ship	στο πλοίο	sto plío
once	μια φορά	mya forá
one-way traffic	μονόδρομος	monódhromos
onion	το κρεμμύδι	to kremídhi
open	ανοιχτός	anichtós
open (verb)	ανοίγω	anígho
opera	η όπερα	i ópera
operate	εγχειρίζω	engchirízo
operator (telephone)	η τηλεφωνήτρια	i tilefonítria
operetta	η οπερέτα	i operéta
opposite	απέναντι	apénandi
opposite to	αντίκρυ σε	andíkri se
optician	ο οπτικός	o optikós
orange	το πορτοκάλι	to portokáli
orange juice	ο χυμός πορτοκαλιού	o himós portokalyóo
orange (coloured)	πορτοκαλής	portokalís
order (noun, e.g. a meal)	η παραγγελία	i parangelía
order (verb, e.g. a meal)	παραγγέλνω	parangélno
others	άλλοι	áli

Word list

15

out of order	χαλασμένος	chalazménos
outside	έξω	éxo
overnight duty	η διανυκτέρευση	i dhianiktérefsi
overtake	προσπερνάω	prospernáo
oysters	τα στρείδια	ta strídhya

P

packed lunch	το πακέτο του μεσημεριανού φαγητού	to pakéto too mesimeryanóo fayitóo
page	η σελίδα	i selídha
pain	ο πόνος	o pónos
pain-killer	το παυσίπονο	to pafsípono
paint	η μπογιά	i boyá
painting (art of)	η ζωγραφική	i zoghrafikí
painting (object)	ο πίνακας	o pínakas
palace	το παλάτι	to paláti
pan	η κατσαρόλα	i katsaróla
pane of glass	το τζάμι	to dzámi
panty liner	η μικρή πετσέτα υγείας	i mikrí petséta iyías
paper	το χαρτί	to chartí
paraffin oil	το πετρέλαιο	to petréleo
parasol	η ομπρέλα	i ombréla
parcel	το δέμα	to dhéma
pardon	συγγνώμη	signómi
parents	οι γονείς	i ghonís
park (verb)	παρκάρω	parkáro
park	το πάρκο	to párko
parliament (building)	η βουλή	i voolí
parsley	ο μαϊντανός	o maidanós
partner	ο/η σύζυγος	o/i sízighos
party	το πάρτυ	to párti
passable (road or stream)	βατός	vatós
passenger	ο επιβάτης	o epivátis
passport photograph	η φωτογραφία διαβατηρίου	i fotoghrafía dhiavatiríoo
passport	το διαβατήριο	to dhiavatíryo
patient	ο ασθενής	o asthenís
pavement	το πεζοδρόμιο	to pezodhrómio
pay the bill	πληρώνω	pliróno
pay (verb)	πληρώνω	pliróno
pea	ο αρακάς	o arakás
peach	το ροδάκινο	to rodhákino
peanuts	τα φιστίκια	ta fistíkya
pear	το αχλάδι	to achládhi
pedestrian crossing	η διάβαση πεζών	i dhiávasi pezón
pedicure	το πεντικιούρ	to pedikyóor
pen	το στυλό	to stiló
pencil	το μολύβι	to molívi
penis	το πέος	to péos
pension	η σύνταξη	i síndaxi
pepper	το πιπέρι	to pipéri
pepper (vegetable)	η πιπεριά	i piperyá
performance	η παράσταση	i parástasi
perfume	το άρωμα	to ároma
perm (verb)	κάνω περμανάντ	káno permanánt
permanent wave	η περμανάντ	i permanánt
permit	η άδεια	i ádhya

person	το άτομο	to átomo
personal	προσωπικός	prosopikós
petrol	η βενζίνη	i venzíni
petrol (high-octane)	η σούπερ	i sóoper
petrol station	το βενζινάδικο	to venzinádhiko
pets	τα κατοικίδια ζώα	ta katikídhia zóa
phone number	ο αριθμός	o arithmós
phone (verb)	τηλεφωνώ	tilefonó
phone book	ο τηλεφωνικός κατάλογος	o tilefonikós katáloghos
phone	το τηλέφωνο	to tiléfono
phone box	ο τηλεφωνικός θάλαμος	o tilefonikós thálamos
photocopier	το φωτοτυπικό μηχάνημα	to fototipikó michánima
photocopy (verb)	κάνω φωτοαντίγραφο	káno fotoandígrafo
photocopy	το φωτοαντίγραφο	to fotoandígrafo
photograph	η φωτογραφία	i fotoghrafía
pick up	παίρνω	pérno
picnic	το πικνίκ	to pikník
pier	η προκυμαία	i prokiméa
pigeon	το περιστέρι	to peristéri
pill	το χάπι	to chápi
pillow	το μαξιλάρι	to maxilári
pillow-case	η μαξιλαροθήκη	i maxilarothíki
pin	η καρφίτσα	i karfítsa
pineapple	ο ανανάς	o ananás
pipe	η πίπα	i pípa
pipe tobacco	ο καπνός για την πίπα	o kapnós ya timbípa
pity	κρίμα	kríma
place of entertainment	το κέντρο	to kéndro
place	ο τόπος	o tópos
place of interest	το αξιοθέατο	to axiotheáto
plan	το σχέδιο	to schédhyo
plant	το φυτό	to fitó
plastic bag	η σακούλα	i sakóola
plastic	πλαστικός	plastikós
plate	το πιάτο	to pyáto
platform	η πλατφόρμα, η γραμμή	i platfórma, i ghramí
play	το θεατρικό έργο	to theatrikó érgho
play (verb)	παίζω	pézo
playground	η παιδική χαρά	i pedhikí chará
playing cards	τα χαρτιά	ta chartyá
pleasant	ευχάριστος	efcháristos
please	παρακαλώ	parakaló
pleasure	η απόλαυση	i apólafsi
pleasure (it's a)	χαίρω πολύ	héro polí
pleasure, with	ευχαρίστως	efcharístos
plum	το δαμάσκηνο	to dhamáskino
pocket knife	ο σουγιάς	o sooyás
point	δείχνω	dhíchno
poison	το δηλητήριο	to dhilitírio
police court	το αυτόφωρο	to aftóforo
police	η αστυνομία	i astinomía
police station	το αστυνομικό τμήμα	to astinomikó tmíma
policeman	ο αστυνομικός	o astinomikós

pond	η λιμνούλα	*i limnóola*
pony	το πόνυ	*to póni*
pop concert	η συναυλία ποπ	*i sinavlía pop*
population	ο πληθυσμός	*o plithizmós*
pork	το χοιρινό κρέας	*to hirinó kréas*
port	το λιμάνι	*to limáni*
porter (doorman)	ο θυρωρός	*o thirorós*
porter	ο αχθοφόρος	*o achthofóros*
portion	η μερίδα	*i merídha*
post office	το ταχυδρομείο	*to tahidhromío*
post code	ο ταχυδρομικός	*o tahidhromikós*
	κώδικας	*kódhikas*
post-box	το γραμματοκιβώτιο	*to ghramatokivótyo*
post-card	η καρτ-ποστάλ	*i kartpostál*
postal charges	τα ταχυδρομικά τέλη	*ta tahidhromiká téli*
postman	ο ταχυδρόμος	*o tahidhrómos*
potato	η πατάτα	*i patáta*

R

recovery service	ΕΛΠΑ	*i elpá*
refrigerator	το ψυγείο	*to psiyío*
region	η περιοχή	*i periohí*
registered	συστημένος	*sistiménos*
registration number	ο αριθμός κυκλοφορίας	*o arithmós kikloforías*
reliable	αξιόπιστος	*axiópistos*
religion	η θρησκεία	*i thriskía*
religion	η πίστη	*i písti*
rent out	νοικιάζω	*nikyázo*
repair (verb)	επιδιορθώνω	*epidhiorthóno*
repairs	η επιδιόρθωση	*i epidhiórthosi*
repeat	επαναλαμβάνω	*epanalamváno*
responsible	υπεύθυνος	*ipéfthinos*
rest	ξεκουράζομαι	*xekoorázome*
restaurant	το εστιατόριο	*to estiatório*
retired	συνταξιούχος	*sintaxióochos*
return (ticket)	μετ' επιστροφής	*metepistrofís*
reverse	κάνω όπισθεν	*káno ópisthen*
rheumatism	ο ρευματισμός	*o revmatizmós*
rice	το ρύζι	*to rízi*
riding school	η σχολή ιππασίας	*i scholí ipasías*
riding (horseback)	η ιππασία	*i ipasía*
right of way	η προτεραιότητα	*i protereótita*
right	δεξιά	*dhexyá*
right, on the	δεξιά	*dhexyá*
ripe	ώριμος	*órimos*
river	το ποτάμι	*to potámi*
road suitable for cars	ο αυτοκινητόδρομος	*o aftokinitódhromos*
roasted	ψημένος	*psiménos*
rock	ο βράχος	*o vráchos*
roof (flat)	η ταράτσα	*i tarátsa*
roof-rack	η σχάρα αυτοκινήτου	*i schára aftokinítoo*
room service	η εξυπηρέτηση	*i exipirétisi dhomatíoo*
	δωματίου	
room number	ο αριθμός δωματίου	*o arithmós dhomatíoo*
room	το δωμάτιο	*to dhomátyo*
rope	το σκοινί	*to skiní*
rosé wine	κρασί ροζέ	*krasí rozé*

roundabout	η ροτόντα	i rotónda
route	η πορεία	i poría
rowing boat	η βάρκα	i várka
rubber	το λάστιχο	to lásticho
rucksack	το σακίδιο	to sakídhyo
rude	αγενής	ayenís
ruins	τα ερείπια	ta erípya
run into	συναντώ	sinandó

S

sad	θλιμμένος	thliménos
safe	ασφαλής	asfalís
safe (deposit box)	το χρηματοκιβώτιο	to chrimatokivótyo
safety pin	η παραμάνα	i paramána
sail	αρμενίζω	armenízo
sailing boat	το ιστιοφόρο	to istiofóro
salad oil	το λάδι	to ládhi
salad	η σαλάτα	i saláta
salami	το σαλάμι	to salámi
sale	το ξεπούλημα	to xepóolima
salt	το αλάτι	to aláti
same	ο ίδιος	o ídhyos
sandy beach	η πλαζ	i plaz
sanitary pad	η πετσέτα υγείας	i petséta iyías
sardines	οι σαρδέλες	i sardhéles
satisfied	πολύ ευχαριστημένος/η	polí efcharistiménos/i
Saturday	το Σάββατο	to sávato
sauce	η σάλτσα	i sáltsa
sauna	η σάουνα	i sáoona
sausage	το λουκάνικο	to lookániko
savoury	πικάντικος	pikándikos
say	λέγω	légho
scarf	το κασκόλ	to kaskól
scenic walk	η βόλτα	i vólta
school	το σχολείο	to scholío
scissors	το ψαλίδι	to psalídhi
scooter	η βεσπα	i véspa
scorpion	ο σκορπιός	o skorpyós
Scotland	η Σκωτία	i skotía
Scotsman/woman	ο Σκωτσέζος/η Σκωτσέζα	o skotsézos/ i skotséza
scrambled eggs	η στραπατσάδα	i strapatsádha
screw	η βίδα	i vídha
screwdriver	το κατσαβίδι	to katsavídhi
sculpture	η γλυπτική	i ghliptikí
sea	η θάλασσα	i thálasa
search	ψάχνω	psáchno
search for	ψάχνω	psáchno
seasickness	η ναυτία	i naftía
seat	η θέση	i thési
seatbelt	η ζώνη	i zóni
second	δεύτερος	dhéfteros
second (of time)	το δευτερόλεπτο	to dhefterólepto
second-hand	μεταχειρισμένος	metahirizménos
secretion	η έκκριση	i ékrisi
sedative	το ηρεμιστικό	to iremistikó
see	βλέπω	vlépo

Word list

15

self-timer (photo)	ο αυτορρυθμιζόμενος φωτοφράκτης	o aftorithmizómenos fotofráktis
semi-skimmed	ημίπαχο	imípacho
send	στέλνω	stélno
sentence	η πρόταση	i prótasi
September	ο Σεπτέμβριος	o septémvrios
serious	σοβαρός	sovarós
service	η εξυπηρέτηση	i exipirétisi
shade	ο ίσκιος	o ískyos
shallow	ρηχός	richós
shampoo	το σαμπουάν	to sampwán
shark	ο καρχαρίας	o karcharías
shave (verb)	ξυρίζω	xirízo
shaver	η ξυριστική μηχανή	i xiristikí michaní
shaving soap	το σαπούνι ξυρίσματος	to sapóoni xirízmatos
shaving brush	το πινέλο ξυρίσματος	to pinélo xirízmatos
shaving cream	η κρέμα ξυρίσματος	i kréma xirízmatos
sheet	το σεντόνι	to sendóni
sherry	το σέρυ	to séri
shirt	το πουκάμισο	to pookámiso
shoe	το παπούτσι	to papóotsi
shoe shop	το υποδηματοπωλείο, το παπουτσάδικο	to ipodhimatopolío, to papootsádhiko
shoe polish	το βερνίκι παπουτσιών	to verníki papootsyón
shoelace	το κορδόνι	to kordhóni
shop assistant	η πωλήτρια	i polítria
shop	το μαγαζί	to maghazí
shop window	η βιτρίνα	i vitrína
shop	ψωνίζω	psonízo
shopping centre	το εμπορικό κέντρο	to emborikó kéndro
short circuit	το βραχυκύκλωμα	to vrachikíkloma
short	κοντός	kondós
shortly	σε λίγο	se lígho
shoulder	ο ώμος	o ómos
show	η παράσταση	i parástasi
shower	το ντους	to doos
shutter	το παντζούρι	to padzóori
sick	άρρωστος	árostos
side of the street	η μεριά του δρόμου	i meryá too dhrómoo
sieve	το σουρωτήρι	to soorotíri
sign (verb)	υπογράφω	ipoghráfo
sign	η πινακίδα	i pinakídha
signature	η υπογραφή	i ipoghrafí
silence	η ησυχία	i isihía
silver	το ασήμι	to asími
silver-plated	επάργυρος	epáryiros
simple	απλός	aplós
single (ticket)	απλό εισιτήριο	apló isitírio
single (unmarried)	ανύπανδρος	anípandhros
single	μονός	monós
sister	η αδερφή	i adherfí
sit	κάθομαι	káthome
size	το νούμερο	to nóomero
skating	το πατινάζ	to patináz
skin rash	το εξάνθημα	to exánthima
skin	το δέρμα	to dhérma
skirt	η φούστα	i fóosta

sleep	κοιμάμαι	kimáme
sleeping pills	τα υπνωτικά	ta ipnotiká
sleeping car	το βαγκον-λί	to vagonlí
slides	τα σλάιτς	ta sláidz
slip (woman's)	το μεσοφόρι	to mesofóri
slow train	το αργό τρένο	to arghó tréno
small	μικρός	mikrós
small change	τα ψηλά	ta psilá
smell of (verb)	βρομώ	vromó
smoke	ο καπνός	o kapnós
smoke (verb)	καπνίζω	kapnízo
smoked	καπνιστός	kapnistós
smoking compartment	το βαγόνι καπνίσματος	to vaghóni kapnízmatos
snake	το φίδι	to fídhi
snorkel	ο αναπνευστήρας	o anapnevstíras
snow	το χιόνι	to hyóni
snowing, it is	χιονίζει	hyonízi
soap powder	η σαπουνόσκονη	i sapoonóskoni
soap	το σαπούνι	to sapóoni
soap dish	η σαπουνιέρα	i sapoonyéra
socket	η πρίζα	i príza
socks	οι κάλτσες	i káltses
soft drink	το αναψυκτικό	to anapsiktikó
soft toy	το ζωάκι (παιδιού)	to zoáki (pedhyóo)
sole	η σόλα	i sóla
sole (fish)	η γλώσσα	i ghlósa
someone	κάποιος	kápyos
sometimes	μερικές φορές	merikés forés
somewhere	κάπου	kápoo
son	ο γιος	o yos
soon	γρήγορα	ghríghora
sore throat	ο πονόλαιμος	o ponólemos
sorry	λυπάμαι	lipáme
sort/type	το είδος	to ídhos
soup	η σούπα	i sóopa
sour	ξινός	xinós
source	η πηγή	i piyí
south wind	ο νοτιάς	o notyás
souvenir	το σουβενίρ	to soovenír
spaghetti	τα μακαρόνια	ta makarónya
spanner	το γαλλικό κλειδί	to ghalikó klidhí
spare tyre	η ρεζέρβα	i rezérva
spare wheel	η ρόδα ρεζέρβα	i ródha rezérva
spare	η ρεζέρβα	i rezérva
spare	το ανταλλακτικό	to andalaktikó
spare parts	τα εξαρτήματα ρεζέρβας	ta exartímata rezérvas
speak	μιλάω	miláo
special	εξαιρετικός	exeretikós
specialist	ο ειδικός	o idhikós
speciality	η σπεσιαλιτέ	i spesialité
speed limit	η ανώτατη ταχύτητα	i anótati tahítita
spell	συλλαβίζω	silavízo
spicy	πικάντικος	pikándikos
splinter	η αγκίδα	i angídha
spoon	το κουτάλι	to kootáli
sport	ο αθλητισμός	o athlitizmós

Word list

15

sports centre	το αθλητικό κέντρο	to athlitikó kéndro
sportsground	το γήπεδο	to yípedho
sprain	στραμπουλίζω	stramboolízo
spring	η άνοιξη	i ánixi
square	η πλατεία	i platía
square (shape)	το τετράγωνο	to tetrághono
square metre	το τετραγωνικό μέτρο	to tetraghonikó métro
squeeze (verb)	ζουλώ	zooló
stain	ο λεκές	o lekés
stairs	η σκάλα	i skála
stalls (theatre)	η πλατεία	i platía
stamp	το γραμματόσημο	to ghramatósimo
start	παίρνω μπρος	pérno bros
station	ο σταθμός	o stathmós
statue	το άγαλμα	to ághalma
stay	η διαμονή	i dhiamoní
stay (verb)	μένω	méno
steal	κλέβω	klévo
steel	το ατσάλι	to atsáli
stench	η μπόχα	i bócha
sticking plaster	ο λευκοπλάστης	o lefkoplástis
sting (verb)	τσιμπάω	tsimbáo
stitch (verb)	ράβω	rávo
stitches (medical)	τα ράμματα	ta rámata
stockings	οι κάλτσες	i káltses
stomachache	ο στομαχόπονος	o stomachóponos
stomach cramp	η κράμπα στην κοιλιά	i krámpa stingilía
stomach	το στομάχι	to stomáchi
stools (medical)	τα κόπρανα	ta kóprana
stop	σταματάω	stamatáo
stop	η στάση	i stási
stopover	η ενδιάμεση προσγείωση	i endhiámesi prosyíosi
storm, there is a	έχει τρικυμία	ehí trikimía
storm	η θύελλα	i thíela
straight hair	ίσια μαλλιά	ísya malyá
straight ahead	ίσια	ísya
straw	το καλαμάκι	to kalamáki
strawberries	οι φράουλες	i fráooles
street	ο δρόμος, η οδός	o dhrómos, i odhós
strike	η απεργία	i aperyía
stroll around town	η βόλτα στην πόλη	i vólta stimbóli
strong	δυνατός	dhinatós
study	σπουδάζω	spoodházo
stuffing	η γέμιση	i yémisi
subtitled	με υπότιτλους	me ipotítloos
succeed	τα καταφέρνω	ta kataférno
sugar	η ζάχαρη	i záchari
sugar cubes	οι κύβοι ζάχαρης	i kívi zácharis
suit	το κοστούμι	to kostóomi
suitcase	η βαλίτσα	i valítsa
summer time	η καλοκαιρινή ώρα	i kalokyeriní óra
summer	το καλοκαίρι	to kalokyéri
sun hat	το καπέλο ηλίου	to kapélo ilíoo
sun	ο ήλιος	o ílyos
sunbathing	η ηλιοθεραπεία	i ilyotherapía
Sunday	η Κυριακή	i kiryakí

sunglasses	τα μαύρα γυαλιά	*ta mávra yalyá*
sunrise	η ανατολή	*i anatolí*
sunset	το ηλιοβασίλεμα	*to ilyovasílema*
sunstroke	η ηλίαση	*i ilíasi*
suntan lotion	η κρέμα ηλίου	*i kréma ilíoo*
suntan oil	το λάδι ηλίου	*to ládhi ilíoo*
supermarket	η υπεραγορά	*i iperaghorá*
surcharge	το συμπληρωματικό ποσόν	*to simpliromatikó posón*
surf board	η σανίδα του σερφ	*i sanídha too serf*
surfing	το σέρφιγκ	*to sérfing*
surname	το επώνυμο	*to epónimo*
surprise	η έκπληξη	*i ékplixi*
swallow (verb)	καταπίνω	*katapíno*
swamp	το τέλμα	*to télma*
sweat	ο ιδρώτας	*o idhrótas*
sweet	γλυκός	*ghlikós*
sweetcorn	το καλαμπόκι	*to kalambóki*
sweets	οι καραμέλες	*i karaméles*
swim (verb)	κολυμπώ	*kolimbó*
swimming pool	η πισίνα	*i pisína*
swimming costume	το μαγιό	*to mayó*
swindle	η απάτη	*i apáti*
switch	ο διακόπτης	*o dhiakóptis*
synagogue	η συναγωγή	*i sinaghoyí*

T

table	το τραπέζι	*to trapézi*
table tennis	το πινγκ πονγκ	*to ping pong*
tablet	το χάπι	*to chápi*
take (photograph)	βγάζω	*vgházo*
take	παίρνω	*pérno*
take (verb, of time)	διαρκώ/κρατώ	*dhiarkó/krató*
take pictures	φωτογραφίζω	*fotoghrafízo*
talcum powder	το ταλκ	*to talk*
talk	μιλάω	*miláo*
tampon	το ταμπόν	*to tampón*
tap water	το νερό της βρύσης	*to neró tis vrísis*
tap	η βρύση	*i vrísi*
taste	δοκιμάζω	*dhokimázo*
tasty	νόστιμος	*nóstimos*
tax-free shop	το μαγαζί αφορολόγητων ειδών	*to maghazí aforolóyiton idhón*
taxi	το ταξί	*to taxí*
taxi stand	η στάση ταξί	*i stási taxí*
teaspoon	το κουταλάκι	*to kootaláki*
tea	το τσάι	*to tsái*
teapot	η τσαγιέρα	*i tsayéra*
tee shirt	η φανέλα	*i fanéla*
telegram	το τηλεγράφημα	*to tileghráfima*
telephone receiver	το ακουστικό	*to akoostikó*
telephone number	ο αριθμός τηλεφώνου	*o arithmós tilefónoo*
telescopic lens	ο τηλεφακός	*o tilefakós*
television	η τηλεόραση	*i tileórasi*
telex	το τηλέτυπο	*to tilétipo*
temperature	η θερμοκρασία	*i thermokrasía*

Word list

15

temporary filling	το προσωρινό σφράγισμα	to prosorinó sfráyizma
temporary	προσωρινός	prosorinós
tender	μαλακός	malakós
tennis ball	η μπάλα του τένις	i bála too ténis
tennis	το τένις	to ténis
tennis racket	η ρακέτα του τένις	i rakéta too ténis
tennis court	το γήπεδο τένις	to yípedho ténis
tent	η σκηνή	i skiní
tent peg	το πασαλάκι της σκηνής	to pasaláki tis skinís
terrible	φοβερός	foverós
thank you	ευχαριστώ	efcharistó
thank (verb)	ευχαριστώ	efcharistó
thaw	λιώνω	lióno
the same	το ίδιο	to ídhyo
theatre	το θέατρο	to théatro
theft	η κλοπή	i klopí
there	εκεί	ekí
thermometer	το θερμόμετρο	to thermómetro
thick	χοντρός	chondrós
thief	ο κλέφτης	o kléftis
thigh	το μπούτι	to bóoti
thin	λεπτός, αδύνατος	leptós, adhínatos
things	τα πράματα	ta prámata
think (verb)	νομίζω	nomízo
third	το τρίτο	to tríto
thirst	η δίψα	i dhípsa
this morning	σήμερα το πρωί	símera to proí
this evening	απόψε	apópse
this afternoon	σήμερα το απόγευμα	símera to apóyevma
thread	η κλωστούλα, η κλωστή	i klostóola, i klostí
throat lozenges	οι παστίλιες για το λαιμό	i pastílyes ya to lemó
throat	ο λαιμός	o lemós
throw up (be sick)	κάνω εμετό	káno emetó
thunderstorm	η καταιγίδα	i kateyídha
Thursday	η Πέμπτη	i pémpti
ticket	το εισιτήριο	to isitírio
tidy up (verb)	μαζεύω	mazévo
tie	η γραβάτα	i ghraváta
tights	το καλτσόν	to kaltsón
time	η ώρα	i óra
times	φορές	forés
timetable	το δρομολόγιο	to dhromolóyo
tinned food	η κονσέρβα	i konsérva
tip	το πουρμπουάρ	to poorbwáar
tissues	τα χαρτομάντηλα	ta chartomándila
to let	νοικιάζεται	nikyázete
toast (French-style)	η φρυγανιά	i frighanyá
tobacco	ο καπνός	o kapnós
tobacco (loose)	ο καπνός	o kapnós
tobacconist's	το καπνοπωλείο	to kapnopolío
today	σήμερα	símera
toe	το δάχτυλο	to dháchtilo
together	μαζί	mazí

toilet	η τουαλέτα	i twaléta
toilet paper	το χαρτί υγείας	to chartí iyías
toiletries	τα είδη τουαλέτας	ta ídhi twalétas
tomato puree	ο ντοματοπολτός	o domatopoltós
tomato	η ντομάτα	i domáta
tomato sauce	το κέτσαπ	to kétsap
tomorrow	αύριο	ávrio
tongue	η γλώσσα	i ghlósa
tonic water	το τόνικ	to tónik
tonight	απόψε	apópse
too	επίσης	epísis
tooth	το δόντι	to dhóndi
toothache	ο πονόδοντος	o ponódhondos
toothbrush	η οδοντόβουρτσα	i odhondóvoortsa
toothpaste	η οδοντόπαστα	i odhondópasta
toothpick	η οδοντογλυφίδα	i odhondoghlifídha
torch	ο φακός	o fakós
total	το σύνολο	to sínolo
tough	σκληρός	sklirós
tour guide	ο ξεναγός	o xenaghós
tour boat	το εκδρομικό καραβάκι	to ekdhromikó karaváki
tourist card	η τουριστική κάρτα	tooristikí kárta
tourist class	η τουριστική θέση	i tooristikí thési
tourist menu	το τουριστικό μενού	to tooristikó menóo
Tourist Information Office	το τουριστικό γραφείο	to tooristikó ghrafío
tow rope	το σκοινί τραβήγματος	to skiní travíghmatos
tow	τραβάω	traváo
towel	η πετσέτα	i petséta
tower	ο πύργος	o pírghos
town-hall	το δημαρχείο	to dhimarchío
toys	τα παιχνίδια	ta pechnídhya
traffic light	το φανάρι	to fanári
traffic	η κυκλοφορία	i kikloforía
train ticket	το εισιτήριο τρένου	to isitírio trénoo
train	το τρένο	to tréno
trainers	τα παπούτσια αθλητισμού	ta papóotsya athlitizmóo
translate	μεταφράζω	metafrázo
travel agent	το πρακτορείο ταξιδίων	to praktorío taxidhíon
travel	ταξιδεύω	taxidhévo
traveller	ο ταξιδιώτης	taxidhyótis
traveller's cheque	η ταξιδιωτική επιταγή	i taxidhyotikí epitayí
treacle	το σιρόπι	to sirópi
treatment	η θεραπεία	i therapía
triangle	το τρίγωνο	to tríghono
trim (verb)	ψαλιδίζω	psalidhízo
trip	το ταξίδι	to taxídhi
trousers	το παντελόνι	to pandelóni
trout	η πέστροφα	i péstrofa
trunk (call)	υπεραστικός	iperastikós
try on	δοκιμάζω	dhokimázo
tube	το σωληνάριο	to solinário
Tuesday	η Τρίτη	i tríti
tumble drier	το στεγνωτήριο	to steghnotírio
tuna	ο τόννος	o tónos

Word list

15

tunnel	το τούνελ	to tóonel
TV guide	ο οδηγός ραδιοφώνου/	o odhighós
	τηλεόρασης	radhiofónoo/tileórasis
tweezers	το τσιμπιδάκι	to tsimbidháki
tyre	το εξωτερικό λάστιχο	to exoterikó lásticho
tyre pressure	η πίεση λάστιχων	i píesi lástichon
tyre lever	ο μοχλός για την	o mochlós ya tin aféresi
	αφαίρεση λάστιχων	lástichon

U

ugly	άσχημος	áschimos
ulcer	το έλκος	to élkos
umbrella	η ομπρέλα	i ombréla
under	κάτω από	káto apó
underground	το μετρό	to metró
underground train system	το δίκτυο του μετρό	to dhíktio too metró
underground station	ο σταθμός του μετρό	o stathmós too metró
underpants (ladies')	το σλιπάκι	to slipáki
underpants	το σώβρακο	to sóvrako
understand	καταλαβαίνω	katalavéno
underwear	τα εσώρουχα	ta esóroocha
undress	γδύνω	ghdhíno
unemployed	άνεργος	ánerghos
uneven	άνισος	ánisos
university	το πανεπιστήμιο	to panepistímio
unleaded	αμόλυβδος	amólivdhos
urgency	η βιασύνη	i viasíni
urgent	επείγον	epíghon
urine	τα ούρα	ta óora
use (verb)	χρησιμοποιώ	chrisimopyó
usually	συνήθως	siníthos
utensil (cooking)	το σκεύος	to skévos

V

vacate	αδειάζω	adhyázo
vaccinate	εμβολιάζω	emvolyázo
vagina	ο κόλπος	o kólpos
vaginal infection	η κολπική μόλυνση	i kolpikí mólinsi
valid	έγκυρος	éngkiros
valley	η κοιλάδα, το λαγκάδι	i kiládha, to langádhi
valuable	πολύτιμος	polítimos
van	το φορτηγάκι	to fortigháki
vanilla	η βανίλια	i vanílya
vase	το βάζο	to vázo
vaseline	η βαζελίνη	i vazelíni
veal	το μοσχαρίσιο κρέας	to moscharísyo kréas
vegetable soup	η χορτόσουπα	i chortósoopa
vegetables	τα λαχανικά	ta lachaniká
vegetarian	ο χορτοφάγος	o chortofághos
vein	η φλέβα	i fléva
venereal disease	το αφροδίσιο νόσημα	to afrodhísyo nósima
vest	η φανέλλα	i fanéla
via	μέσω	méso
video recorder	το βίντεο	to vídeo
videotape	η βιντεοταινία	i videotenía
view	η θέα	i théa

English	Greek	Transliteration
village festival/fair	το πανηγύρι	to paniyíri
village woman	η χωριάτισσα	i choriátisa
village	το χωριό	to choryó
viral infection	η ίωση	i íosi
visa	η βίζα	i víza
visit	η επίσκεψη	i epískepsi
visit (verb)	επισκέπτομαι	episképtome
visiting time	η ώρα επίσκεψης	i óra epísképsis
vitamin pills	τα χάπια βιταμίνης	ta chápya vitamínis
vitamin	η βιταμίνη	i vitamíni
volcano	το ηφαίστειο	to iféstio
volleyball	το βόλλεϋ	to vólei
vomit	κάνω εμετό	káno emetó

W

wait for	περιμένω	periméno
waiter	το γκαρσόνι	to garsóni
waiting room	η αίθουσα αναμονής	i éthoosa anamonís
waitress	η σερβιτόρα	i servitóra
wake up	ξυπνάω	xipnáo
Wales	η Ουαλλία	i walia
walk	ο περίπατος	o perípatos
walk (verb)	περπατώ	perpató
wallet	το πορτοφόλι	to portofóli
wardrobe	η γκαρντ-ρόμπα	i gard-róba
warm	θερμός, ζεστός	thermós, zestós
warn	προειδοποιώ	proidhopió
warning	η προειδοποίηση	i proidhopíisi
wash	πλένω	pléno
washing machine	το πλυντήριο	to plindírio
washing	η μπουγάδα	i booghádha
washing powder	το απορρυπαντικό	to aporipandikó
washing line	το σκοινί μπουγάδας	to skiní booghádhas
wasp	η σφήκα	i sfíka
water	το νερό	to neró
water-ski	το θαλάσσιο σκι	to thalásio ski
waterfall	ο καταρράχτης	o kataráchtis
waterproof	αδιάβροχος	adhiávrochos
wave-pool	πισίνα με κύματα	pisína me kímata
waves	τα κύματα	ta kímata
way (road)	ο δρόμος	o dhrómos
way	η κατεύθυνση	i katéfthinsi
way, on the	στο δρόμο	sto dhrómo
we	εμείς	emís
weak	αδύνατος	adhínatos
weather	ο καιρός	o kyerós
weather forecast	το μετεωρολογικό δελτίο	to meteoroloyikó dheltío
wedding	ο γάμος	o ghámos
Wednesday	η Τετάρτη	i tetárti
week	η εβδομάδα	i evdhomádha
weekend	το σαββατοκύριακο	to savatokíryako
weekly ticket	η εβδομαδιαία κάρτα	evdhomadhiéa kárta
welcome	καλώς ήρθατε	kalós írthate
well done (cooking)	καλοψημένος	kalopsiménos
well	καλά	kalá
well	καλός	kalós

west (to the)	δυτικά	*dhitiká*
wet	υγρός	*ighrós*
wet-suit	το κοστούμι του σερφ	*to kostóomi too serf*
what?	τί;	*ti?*
wheel	η ρόδα	*i ródha*
wheelchair	το καροτσάκι (αναπήρων)	*to karotsáki (anapíron)*
when?	πότε;	*póte?*
where?	πού;	*poo?*
which?	ποιός;	*pyos?*
whipped cream	η σαντιγί	*i santiyí*
white	άσπρος	*áspros*
who?	ποιός;	*pyos?*
why?	γιατί;	*yatí?*
wide-angle lens	ο ευρυγώνιος φακός	*o evrighónyos fakós*
widow	η χήρα	*i híra*
widower	ο χήρος	*o híros*
wife	η γυναίκα	*i yinéka*
wind	ο άνεμος	*o ánemos*
windbreak	ο ανεμοφράκτης	*o anemofráchtis*
window	το παράθυρο	*to paráthiro*
window (booking office, bank)	η θυρίδα	*i thirídha*
wine	το κρασί	*to krasí*
wine list	ο κατάλογος κρασιών	*o katáloghos krasyón*
winter	ο χειμώνας	*o himónas*
witness	ο μάρτυρας	*o mártiras*
woman	η γυναίκα	*i yinéka*
wonderful	θαυμάσιος	*thavmásios*
wood	το ξύλο	*to xílo*
wool	το μαλλί	*to malí*
word	η λέξη	*i léxi*
work	η δουλειά	*i dhoolyiá*
working day	η εργάσιμη ημέρα	*i erghásimi méra*
workout	η άσκηση	*i áskisi*
worn	τριμμένος	*triménos*
worried	ανήσυχος	*anísichos*
wound	η πληγή	*i pliyí*
wrap	τυλίγω	*tilígho*
wrist	ο καρπός	*o karpós*
write	γράφω	*ghráfo*
write down	καταγράφω	*kataghráfo*
writing paper	το χαρτί αλληλογραφίας	*to chartí aliloghrafías*
written document	γραπτά	*ghraptá*
wrong	λάθος	*láthos*

Y

yacht	το γιωτ	*to yot*
year	ο χρόνος	*o chrónos*
yellow	κίτρινος	*kítrinos*
yes	ναι	*ne*
yesterday	χτες	*chtes*
yoghurt	το γιαούρτι	*to yaóorti*
you	εσείς	*esís*
youth hostel	ο ξενώνας νεότητας	*o xenónas neótitas*

Z

| zip | το φερμουάρ | *to fermwár* |
| zoo | ο ζωολογικός κήπος | *o zo-oloyikós kípos* |

Basic grammar

1 The Greek alphabet

(See also 1.8 Telephone alphabet)

α	Α	álfa	somewhere between **a** in **mast** and **u** in **cup**
ß	Β	víta	as **v** in **van**
γ	Γ	gháma	as **y** in **yet** before **e** and **i** sounds; before any other sound, a hard **g** (as in **grab**) as far down your throat as possible. (This sound is shown as **gh** in the transcriptions.)
δ	Δ	dhélta	as hard **th** in **this**
ε	Ε	épsilon	as **e** in **met**
ζ	Ζ	zíta	as **z** in **zoo**
η	Η	íta	as **i** in **quarantine** (i.e. like the **ee** in **feet**)
θ	Θ	thíta	as soft **th** in **thin**
ι	Ι	yóta	as **i** in **quarantine** (i.e. like **ee** in **feet**), but before another vowel often becomes **y-** as in **yacht**)
κ	Κ	kápa	as **k** in **kitchen**, but before **e-** and **i-** sounds, more like **ky**)
λ	Λ	lámdha	as **l** in **lick**
μ	Μ	mi	as **m** in **mat**
ν	Ν	ni	as **n** in **not**
ξ	Ξ	xi	as **x** in **box**
ο	Ο	ómikron	as **o** in **pop**
π	Π	pi	as **p** in **pin**
ρ	Ρ	ro	closer to a Scots **r** than an English one
σ,ς	Σ	síghma	like a soft English **s** as in **sit**, except before the sounds **b,gh,dh** and **m**, when it is like **z**
τ	Τ	taf	as **t** in **tin**
υ	Υ	ípsilon	as **i** in **quarantine** (i.e. like the **ee** in **feet**)
φ	Φ	fi	as **f** in **fit**
χ	Χ	hi	as **h** in **hat** before **i** or **e** sounds; before any other sound, as Scots **ch** in **loch**
ψ	Ψ	psi	as combination of **p** and **s** in **tops**
ω	Ω	omégha	as **o** in **pop**

2 Vowels

There are only five vowels sounds in Greek, approximating to the English sounds a (see α), e (see ε), ee (see ι), o (see o) and oo as in foot (spelt ou), but several of these sounds can be written in a number of ways:

ε, αι both = **e** in **met**

η, ι, υ, ει, οι = **i** in **quarantine** (ie. like **ee** in **feet**)

ο, ω = o in pot

N.B. αυ and ευ are pronounced **av** and **ev** before ß, γ, δ, ζ, λ, μ, ν, ρ, τ or another vowel; before anything else they are pronounced **f**. Thus **αυγό** (egg) is pronounced *avghó* but **απόλαυση** (enjoyment) is pronounced *apólafsi*.

3 The consonant combinations

As well as the single consonant sounds indicated above in the description of the alphabet, there are a number of sounds which can only be written with two consonants together. These are:

b   as in **bet** = μπ
d   as in **dog** = ντ
g   as in **gap** = γκ.

Similarly, when one word ends in the sound n and the next begins with the sound p, t, or k the following changes occur:
τον πατέρα (ton patéra - the father) becomes *tombatéra*
την ταβέρνα (tin tavérna - the taverna) becomes *tindavrna*
τον καταλογο (ton katálogho) becomes *tongatálogho*.

The following combinations of consonants also make particular sounds:
γγ = **ng** as in **sing**
γξ = **n(g)x** – somewhere between **things** and **thinks**
γχ = **n(g)ch** – try pronouncing the middle of **melancholy** with a Scots **ch** after the **n**. Fortunately, the last two combinations are relatively rare!

4 Stress and accents

The accents on Greek words indicate where the stress goes. In the pronunciation guide the stresses are also marked with an accent, e.g. **ο πατέρας** = *o patéras*. The vowel **ou** is transcribed as **oo** when not stressed and **óo** when stressed.
N.B. Any two other vowels together in the transcription must be pronounced separately, e.g. **αεροδρόμιο** must be pronounced *a-e-rodhrómyo*.

5 Nouns

Greek nouns each have a gender, which can be masculine, feminine or neuter. They also have endings which change to show whether they are singular or plural, and whether they are nominative, accusative or genetive case. The nominative case is always used for the subject of an action; the accusative is used for the direct object of an action and after most prepositions (in, to, for etc.); the genetive is used to show possession (of someone or something) or indirect objects (to someone or something).

The most common forms are as follows:
masculine nouns have a singular nominative ending in: **-ος,-ας** or **-ης**
a corresponding plural nominative endings in: **-οι -ες -ες**
feminine nouns have a singular nominative ending in: **-η** or **-α**
a plural nominative ending in: **-ες**
neuter nouns have a singular nominative ending in: **-ο, -ι,** or **-α**
a corresponding plural nominative ending in: **-α, -ια -ατα**

In a brief introduction to Greek grammar it is not possible to give all the details of all the categories of nouns. Here are three common nouns in all the cases of both singular and plural, with the definite article (the):

	masculine singular	masculine plural
nominative (subject case)	ο δρόμος (the road)	οι δρόμοι
accusative (direct object case)	τον δρόμο	τους δρόμους
genitive (indirect object case)	του δρόμου	των δρόμων

	feminine singular	feminine plural
nominative (subject case)	η γυναίκα (woman)	οι γυναίκες
accusative (direct object case)	τη(ν) γυναίκα	τις γυναίκες
genitive (indirect object case)	της γυναίκας	των γυναίκων

	neuter singular	neuter plural
nominative (subject case)	το παιδί (child)	τα παιδιά
accusative (direct object case)	το παιδί	τα παιδιά
genitive (indirect object case)	του παιδιού	ού των παιδιών

N.B. Like nouns the definite article (the) also has, as can be seen from the above examples, three genders and nine cases. It must always agree with its noun in number, gender and case. Christian names, names of countries, days of the week and months all take a definite article in front of them, eg. ο Γιάννης (John), η Αγγλία (England), η Παρασκευή (Friday), ο Μάιος (May).

6 Adjectives

Adjectives in Greek behave like the definite article: they agree in gender, number and case with the noun which they describe. The most common form of adjective has endings which are similar to those of the nouns:

	masc. singular	fem. singular	neut. singular
nominative (subject case)	-ος	-α/-η	-ο
accusative (direct object case)	-ο	-α/-η	-ο
genetive (indirect object case)	-ου	-ας/-ης	-ου

	masc. plural	fem. plural	neut. plural
nominative (subject case)	-οι	-ες	-α
accusative (direct object case)	-ους	-ες	-α
genetive (indirect object case)	-ων	-ων	-ων

Adjectives usually stand before their noun, as in English.
The words **αυτός** (this) and **εκείνος** (that) also function as adjectives, but they stand before the definite article. So this beautiful house and of that beautiful woman in Greek are: **αυτό το ωραίο σπίτι** and **εκείνης της ωραίας γυναίκας.**

7 Verbs

Verbs in Greece are very complex. They are made up of two parts: the stem, which gives the main idea of the verb (eg. have, want, drink), and the ending, which shows whether the action is singular or plural, first, second or third person, and past or present. So in the verb **πληρώνω** (pay), the stem is **πληρών-** (the idea of payment) and the ending **-ω** shows that the action is first person singular and present tense. There are two stems for most verbs, and also different sets of endings for active and passive. It is obviously not possible to give more than very basic information in a brief introduction like this. Below is the present tense (active) of the verbs **έχω** (have) and **Θέλω** (want), divided up to show the standard endings.

I have	**έχ-ω**	(écho)	I want	**Θέλ-ω**	(thélo)
You have	**έχ-εις**	(éhis)	You want	**Θέλ-εις**	(thélis)
He/she/it has	**έχ-ει**	(éhi)	He/she/it wants	**Θέλ-ει**	(théli)
We have	**έχ-ουμε**	(échoome)	We want	**Θέλ-ουμε**	(théloome)
You have	**έχ-ετε**	(éhete)	You want	**Θέλ-ετε**	(thélete)
They have	**έχ-ουν**	(échoon)	They want	**Θέλ-ουν**	(théloon)

8 Personal pronouns

As we have seen no separate word for I, you, we etc. is necessary to show the subject of an action, as the ending of the verb gives you this information. The object forms of the personal pronoun are as follows: me = **με**, you (sing.) = **σε**, him = **τον**, her = **τη**, it = **τον, τη** or **το** (according to the gender) we = **μας**, you (plur.) = **σας**, they = **τους** (for people) or **τους** or **τα** (for things). These forms stand before the verb, eg. **το Θέλω** (I want it). To say my, your, his etc., use the following forms after the noun: my = **μου**, your (sing.) = **σου**, his = **του**, her = **της**, our = **μας**, your (plur.) = **σας**, their = **τους** (for people and things): eg. **τα παιδιά μας** = our children.

9 Prepositions

The most common prepositions are **για** (for), **από** (from) and **σε** (in or to). They are all followed by the accusative case, eg. **από την Αθήνα** (from Athens), **για τον φίλο μου** (for my friend). The preposition **σε** contracts with the definite article in the following ways: **σε+τον = στον**, **σε+την = στην**, **σε+το = στο**, eg. **στο Λονδίνο** (in London).